T0129197

# FASHION FIGURES

## HOW MISSY THE MATHLETE MADE THE CUT

*Written by Melissa A. Borza*
*Illustrated by John M. Borza*

**ca** technologies

**CA Press**

Apress®

*Fashion Figures: How Missy the Mathlete Made the Cut*

Melissa A. Borza
River Edge, New Jersey, USA

ISBN-13 (pbk): 978-1-4842-2273-7          ISBN-13 (electronic): 978-1-4842-2274-4
DOI 10.1007/978-1-4842-2274-4

Library of Congress Control Number: 2017952395

Managing Director: Welmoed Spahr
Editorial Director: Todd Green
Acquisitions Editor: Susan McDermott
Development Editor: James Markham
Technical Reviewer: Amy Willoughby-Burle
Illustrator: John M. Borza
Coordinating Editor: Rita Fernando
Copy Editor: Lori Jacobs
Cover: eStudio Calamar

Distributed to the book trade worldwide by Springer Science+Business Media New York, 233 Spring Street, 6th Floor, New York, NY 10013. Phone 1-800-SPRINGER, fax (201) 348-4505, e-mail orders-ny@springer-sbm.com, or visit www.springeronline.com. Apress Media, LLC is a California LLC and the sole member (owner) is Springer Science + Business Media Finance Inc (SSBM Finance Inc). SSBM Finance Inc is a **Delaware** corporation.

For information on translations, please e-mail rights@apress.com, or visit http://www.apress.com/rights-permissions.

Apress titles may be purchased in bulk for academic, corporate, or promotional use. eBook versions and licenses are also available for most titles. For more information, reference our Print and eBook Bulk Sales web page at http://www.apress.com/bulk-sales.

Any source code or other supplementary material referenced by the author in this book is available to readers on GitHub via the book's product page, located at www.apress.com/9781484222737. For more detailed information, please visit http://www.apress.com/source-code.

Printed on acid-free paper

*I dedicate this book to my parents:*
*To my dad, John, for teaching me*
*the art of the story, and to my mom, Edie,*
*for encouraging me to tell my own*
*and to write them down.*

# Contents

# About the Author

**Melissa A. Borza** leads strategy, product management and marketing at a sales enablement software company. Before that, she worked as a product leader at CA Technologies. Prior to that she worked as a journalist and technical writer. Ms. Borza has taught technical writing, public speaking and product management classes and is a member of the Society of Children's Book Writers and Illustrators. She presents regularly at conferences around the world, such as the Grace Hopper Celebration of Women in Computing, and she contributes frequent articles and blogs on change management, team transformations, product management and increasing the representation of women in IT and other STEM careers. Ms. Borza holds a patent in an integrated impact analysis system. She received her MA in Communications from Syracuse University and her BA in English and Psychology from Cornell University.

# About the Illustrator

**John Michael Borza** is a graphic designer and illustrator from Winter Springs, Florida. He has a BA in Fine and Studio Arts from Pfeiffer University. Mr. Borza's art can be found in various galleries and at art shows across Central Florida. Although his training is in traditional media, John has developed a passion for digital drawings and illustrations.

# About the Technical Reviewer

**Amy Willoughby-Burle** is the author of *The Lemonade Year* and *Out Across the Nowhere*. She is a freelance fiction editor and book reviewer. She serves as assistant director of the Wildacres Writers Workshop. She also teaches language arts and creative writing at Elevate Life and Art, an enrichment program for grades K-12 in Asheville, NC. She lives in Candler, NC with her husband, their four children and numerous animals of varying sort. Visit her online at www.amywilloughbyburle.com.

# Acknowledgments

Thank you to CA Technologies and to Apress for publishing this book. I hope it will be a welcome, if unexpected, addition into this technology company's repertoire. Special thanks to Apress's Rita Fernando Kim for her infinite patience and support.

Thank you to my technical editors and reviewers, especially Amy Willoughby-Burle for her candid, caring and helpful feedback.

Thank you to my talented nephew, John Michael Borza, who illustrated most of this book. He is a gifted artist and I am so happy that we could collaborate on this project.

Thank you to girls everywhere who face challenges and persist to embrace science, technology, engineering and math along with fashion, art and design and all the rest of their hearts' desires. My hope is that you will create the world you want to inherit!

Finally, thank you to my husband, Scott Perlowin, and to my three sons, AJ, Christopher and Vincent, who have tolerated not just my rants on this subject but also many evening and weekend absences to allow me to write this book.

# Introduction

The inspiration for this story came to me when researching a blog, I discovered that girls as young as third and fourth graders were opting out of STEM (Science, Technology, Engineering, and Math) tracks. That means that at nine years old, girls are closing career doors they may not even know exist yet. The choices they make have nothing to do with skills or ability but rather are driven by unconsious biases and false assumptions. As we hear more about the dearth of women in tech fields, it's easy to connect the dots. We cannot wait to address this in college or even in high school, as foundational skills for STEM need to be built much earlier. This is a problem that has to be solved in elementary and middle school. Girls need to be encouraged to engage in STEM subjects as early as possible, not just to fill the pipeline but also to drive inclusion and diversity.

This book is written for middle-schoolers facing the pressures of growing up in a hyperconnected, technology-driven universe where traditional social, educational and personal pressures also persist.

This book shows how one girl stuggles with social pressures, varied academic interests and a deep desire to help her friends, family and the world she lives in to be better. She embraces her inner geek, her artistic flair and her heart's true desires to find her way. I hope it inspires more girls to pursue their interests in math AND the arts and to grow their talents to help make our world a better and brighter place for all.

# 104 Driscoll Avenue

The smoky smell of cooking bacon drifted down the hallway of 104 Driscoll Avenue, up three stairs, around a bend, and through Missy's barely cracked door to tickle her nose. *Twelve feet plus three feet plus one and a half feet equals the distance the scent of bacon just traveled from the kitchen.* Missy Maker's brain calculated, as her mouth watered, before she was even fully awake. She let the smell of bacon pull her up into a sitting position and then lead her down the stairs and into her family's kitchen. If G-ma cooks the whole pound . . . *Fifteen slices in one pound of bacon divided by three people, means at least five slices for me.*

G-ma stood with her back toward the counter. She was busy working over the stove, a spatula in one hand and an oversize mug, filled with black coffee and featuring a photo of Missy and her sister, Molly, both smiling widely, in the other. G-ma moved expertly between the frying pan and griddle, her bright blue eyes in stark contrast to her black and silver hair. Missy imagined purple streaks atop G-ma's spiky 'do.

© Melissa A. Borza and CA 2017
M. A. Borza, *Fashion Figures*, DOI 10.1007/978-1-4842-2274-4_1

15 🥓 in a pound
3 🧍 & in Family
so
15 🥓 / 3 🧍
5 🥓 for me!

Bubbles exploded from the tops of the perfect pancake spheres. Missy thought of her favorite ratio—the diameter of a circle to the circumference of a circle—and how it resulted in the irrational and lovely number called pi. In a haze of bacon smoke, the elegant equation for the area of a circle, *pi r-squared,* seemed to float about the stove as G-ma adroitly flipped each pancake over. Just as it was done to crispy perfection, G-ma swiftly removed the bacon strips from the frying pan to a paper-towel covered plate.

"Good morning! Miss Melissa Merry Maker!" G-ma sang out noticing Missy watching her prepare breakfast. Then, as if reading Missy's thoughts, G-ma said, "I cooked only six slices of bacon, dearie. And six pancakes. That's two apiece of each." G-ma winked at Missy who sidled up to the kitchen peninsula and sat on a bar stool.

As Missy watched her grandmother cooking breakfast, she felt an odd weight on her head. She raised her hand and touched her hair. She felt at once that she had forgotten to take down her ponytail before going to bed. Now, it sat askew, leaning to the right and creating a heavy sensation. Missy had unruly frizzy, blond hair. It was long, and Missy found the easiest way to manage it was to wrangle it into a bunch and to tie it tightly atop her head in various positions.

Missy pictured her head as a globe and overlaid a compass in her mind's eye. *Zero degrees at the top; hair slipped to about 70 degrees.* With determination, she grabbed her ponytail, quickly divided the hair between two hands and pulled and wrangled it up to the North Pole. Then Missy gave her hair a sharp tug pulling each handful in opposite directions to lock in the elastic band. Satisfied for now, Missy looked around the kitchen feeling more awake.

Missy's pet cat, Pi, arched its back and weaved in and out of the legs on Missy's stool. As a calico, Missy thought Pi was the most fashionable cat she knew! His brown and black striped fur and green eyes made him ready for any formal event; however, it was the perfectly round patch of black over white fur that encircled his left eye for which she had named him. Missy reached down to stroke Pi's fur.

"What's the occasion, G-ma?" Missy asked sitting back up and resting her chin in her hands.

G-ma plated breakfast for Missy and herself then set down her spatula and delivered the plates to the peninsula. Then she walked to the refrigerator. She took out the maple syrup and butter, then said, "We're celebrating! TGIF: Thank G-ma, it's Friday!"

Missy laughed. *Eighteen days of sixth grade down, one hundred and sixty-two left.*

"Missy!" Mr. Maker called from the hall toward Missy's room.

"In here, Dad," Missy called back, "with G-ma! Breakfast is ready."

Mr. Maker walked into the kitchen and greeted his family. He was dressed as usual wearing a white button-down shirt with a colorful bow tie. Today it was green with yellow polka dots. He also wore his so-called dress-up jeans with black loafers. His black-rimmed glasses dangled precariously from his shirt pocket. "Anyone seen my glasses?" he asked.

"Dad," Missy said, pointing, "they're hanging from your pocket!" Pi watched the exchange carefully and followed Missy's hand to stare up at Mr. Maker, too. He seemed just as incredulous as Missy that Mr. Maker could not find his glasses.

Mr. Maker patted his pocket. Reassured, he asked, "Did you sign up for any clubs last night?" He knew Missy had attended the Cherry Hill Academic Prep School's annual club fair with her best friend AJ, but they hadn't yet talked about it. "I heard from Ms. Jameson that there's a new math club this year and if they have enough students, they can compete in the Math Olympics," Mr. Maker explained.

Ms. Jameson was Missy's math teacher, her neighbor, and her father's childhood friend. *Forty-two minus twelve equals the length of their friendship.* Sometimes it was awkward to have a teacher who your father knew so well. Ms. Jameson was the club advisor and had mentioned the math club to Missy a few times. Her teacher had really tried hard to recruit Missy and her friends to join at the club fair. Now, it seemed Ms. Jameson had also told her dad about it too.

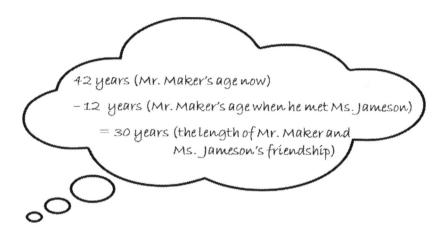

42 years (Mr. Maker's age now)

− 12 years (Mr. Maker's age when he met Ms. Jameson)

= 30 years (the length of Mr. Maker and Ms. Jameson's friendship)

"I signed up for the fashion club with AJ," Missy responded.

G-ma poured steaming black coffee into a travel mug, screwed on the lid, and placed it on the edge of the counter for Mr. Maker. Then she plated the last of the pancakes and bacon and handed it to him.

Mr. Maker sipped his coffee and set the plate down next to Missy's. He raised his eyebrows at Missy who was watching him closely.

"Ha!" she said trying to change the subject away from joining the math club. "You drink too much coffee!"

"Well, I think you'd be a great *addition* to the math club," Mr. Maker joked. "You see what I did there? Math club? Addition?!" He laughed and Missy rolled her eyes. "Think about it, kiddo," he said. "You're great at math and the team could use your skills."

"Sure, Dad," Missy said, knowing that she would never join the math club. It was bad enough she had a brain that automatically invented math stories about everything she looked at! No way did she want her friends to know what a geek she really was. This year, she would shed her childhood nickname, "Missy-Math-Maker," and she would focus on girl stuff. The fashion club was just the ticket! She loved fashion and all the creative possibilities and she knew it would be time-consuming, maybe too time-consuming to do anything else!

Mr. Maker took a gulp of his coffee then looked at his watch. He put his cup down and grabbed a napkin from the napkin holder on the peninsula. He placed one pancake on it; he snapped his bacon into four pieces and added that to the pancake, he topped that with a pat of butter and a drop of syrup, and finally the other pancake; then he rolled his pancake sandwich inside the napkin, swapped it with his glasses in his shirt pocket and grabbed his keys from the counter. He kissed Missy on the forehead before picking up his mug again.

"I want to hear more about this fashion club, kiddo. Have a gee-are-eight day!" he said tugging Missy's ponytail. "See what I did there?" he winked and blew a kiss across the kitchen to G-ma. "Early meeting. I'm off!"

G-ma returned the kiss by air mail then smiled at Missy. "Let's finish up, dearie," she said.

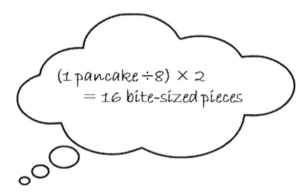

Missy cut her pancakes into quarters then eighths, and calculated how many bite-sized pieces she'd just made. *One bite is one-sixteenth of my pancakes.* She poured maple syrup over her whole plate drenching her pancake pieces and bacon slices. "Did Molly call yet?" she asked G-ma with a mouthful of food.

"Swallow before speaking, dearie. I was just about to check in with her," G-ma said reaching for the kitchen computer keyboard. Just as she clicked the enter key, she heard the familiar dong of a video call coming through.

"Molly!" Missy shouted and positioned herself in front of the screen.

"Good morning Miss Molly May Maker!" said G-ma, using a napkin to touch the screen to peck Molly's cheek as if she were kissing her. "Smooch!" she said.

"Hey, G-ma! Hey, Missy! Did Dad leave?" Molly asked.

"You just missed him," G-ma said.

"Bummer. I wanted to share my news, but I'll send him an email later," Molly said. "You won't believe it! I won a scholarship to go to the Grace Hopper Celebration of Women in Computing!"

Missy wrinkled her nose and peered at her sister through the screen with a confused look on her face. She knew Grace Hopper had been an admiral in the U.S. Navy and an early computer scientist, but why was she having a celebration? "Is it a party?" Missy asked, "Can I come too?"

Molly had been telling G-ma about the program. "It's not a party. It's a conference where thousands of women and men get together and talk about technology! I'm so excited. I'll be counting down the days!"

"That's wonderful, Molly! We are so proud of you!" G-ma said. "Before I retired, I attended a few Grace Hopper events myself! It's a great place to connect and network with folks from a variety of technology areas," G-ma told Molly.

"And maybe I can land a summer internship," Molly added.

G-ma and Molly chatted while Missy finished her breakfast. "Love you, Miss," Molly shouted to Missy as she ended the call. "Let's catch up soon."

Missy missed having her sister at home. *Ten weeks till Molly comes home for break is seventy days or . . .*

Stop! Missy interrupted her thoughts. For a girl who was trying not to be a geek, the message sure hadn't made it to her brain. Missy rinsed her plate in the sink and loaded it into the dishwasher along with her fork and knife. Her mind was racing. How was she ever going to recreate her image as a regular girl if she couldn't even control her own thinking?

Pi pranced to the dishwasher and gave it a sniff. "Ready for breakfast, Pi?" Missy asked. "Tuna or salmon?" Pi wove his way through Missy's legs as Missy got out the can opener and pulled out a can of cat food from the cupboards above. Then she reached down and picked up Pi's dish. She quickly rinsed and dried it and then refilled it. She poured fresh water into his water bowl while Pi actively ignored her. With the bowls filled and replaced in their familiar location, Pi swished his tail and tucked into his own breakfast.

"Fifteen minutes till the bus comes," G-ma reminded Missy. Missy finished feeding Pi and washed her hands in the kitchen sink.

*Fifteen divided by brushing teeth and dressing and walking to the corner to get the bus equals three minutes to brush, two minutes to walk, which leaves ten minutes to dress.* Missy sprinted to the hallway bathroom and brushed her teeth. She ran up the stairs to her room and threw open the doors to her closet. Missy checked her smartphone calendar. "Friday is fun-in-the-sun day," the calendar reminded her.

Missy and her best friend Andrea Jane Dupre, better known as "AJ," had sketched out a fashion calendar for every school day. They had sat down on Missy's bedroom floor and mapped out fashion themes for the first marking period of middle school. Each week had a general theme and every Friday had a specific outfit idea. They typed it all up and posted it online to share with their friends.

As Missy rushed to get ready, she pulled out denim shorts, which at one time had been her favorite jeans. When she had grown two inches over the summer, G-ma had insisted they go into the donations pile. On a lark, Missy cut them off at the knees and frayed the bottom two inches. Now her favorite jeans were her favorite shorts! Missy added a teal t-shirt bejeweled with a sparkly giant M on the front. Next, from her dresser drawer, she took out two knee socks: one black and white striped and one teal with yellow stars.

*Shorts plus top plus sock plus coordinating sock equals one rocking outfit!* Missy dressed quickly and stuffed her feet into her favorite black tennis shoes artfully splattered with reflective pink and orange paint.

She stopped by the full-length mirror in the corner of her room, re-tied her ponytail and put on a pair of teal and glitter cat-eye sunglasses, then she smiled, posed and snapped a selfie. She posted the photo with the hashtags OOTD (Outfit of the Day) and FITSD (Fun-in-the-Sun Day). Satisfied with her look, Missy headed out to catch her bus, shouting "Bye, G-ma," as she pushed through the spring-loaded front door that slammed shut behind her while she scanned her SocialMe feeds to see who else had posted an OOTD.

## MATH HACK: WHAT IS PI?

Pi is an irrational number represented by this symbol from the Greek alphabet:

To calculate pi, you simply divide the circumference of a circle by its diameter. This is also called a ratio. What's so awesome about pi is that it never changes. No matter how large or how small the circle, pi is always the same! Try it for yourself! You'll be amazed.

Here's a trick to help you remember the first digits in pi. Just count the number of letters in each of the words in this phrase: **May I have a large container of coffee?**

When you calculate pi, you will also see that the numbers never repeat or create a pattern. Many people round it down to just the first two decimal places. However, this is pi to its first 100 decimal places:

**3.14**15926535897932384626433832795028841971693993751058209749445923078164062862089986280348253421170679 ...

## FUN FACT

March 14 in the United States is celebrated as Pi Day because March is the third month of the year and this date is notated like this:

**3/14**

# Codes and Crises

Missy saw two things as soon as she rounded the corner of the Sixth Grade Hall at Cherry Hill Academic Prep School or "CHAPS" as it was fondly called. CHAPS was more than just a middle school. It was an entire school campus made of four large buildings including the elementary school or The Lower School and the high school or The Upper School plus an administration building. CHAPS had a reputation, at least among parents, for having strong academics and a great STEM program. STEM stands for science, technology, engineering and math. In her six years in attendance, Missy had come to feel that this was not really the case. In her experience, all the students seemed to care about were sports and popularity; two things she knew nothing about! The CHAPS schools shared a set of offices, a gymnasium, an auditorium, and a cafeteria, which were all housed in the Gates Admin Building, named for a famous and wealthy CHAPS alum, not Bill Gates, though that was one of many school myths that circulated every year. The campus included several sports fields and green areas, and one big, inconvenient, disruptive and unfair rule: no cell phones during school hours. That meant that all cell phones remained locked in lockers or switched off in backpacks all day, every day, no exceptions. Even if they were allowed, as soon as you made it past the main parking area, all signals disappeared and connections dropped. The whole CHAPS campus seemed to be in a bubble of bad reception.

© Melissa A. Borza and CA 2017
M. A. Borza, *Fashion Figures*, DOI 10.1007/978-1-4842-2274-4_2

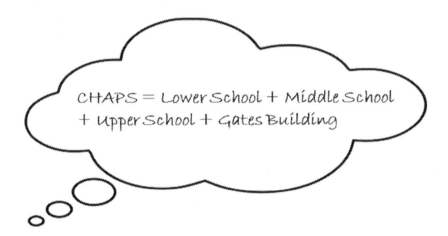

As Missy got closer to her locker, the first thing she noticed was a giant sign that ran the length of the wall: "RED?CE. ?EUSE. RECYCLE. WHAT'S MISSING? U R!"

That brought a smile to Missy's face. She liked codes and puzzles, and that was an easy one! Her smile quickly turned into a pucker when she noticed the second thing.

Missy scrunched her eyebrows and pressed her lips together in concern. The neon green sticky note glittered from the center of her locker. She knew that could mean only one thing—an AJ Dupre crisis!

AJ and Missy had known each other since the first grade in CHAPS, when they met in Mrs. Works' class and sat next to each other. AJ and her family had moved from Pennsylvania to New Jersey when AJ's mom had taken a new job at a pharmaceutical company.

Having a love of puzzles and codes, the two developed many secret languages and various ciphers during elementary school. Missy rarely had occasion to use any of them; meanwhile, AJ had a knack for uncovering urgent scenarios and specific cases to employ their special language.

Missy speed-walked down the hall and peeled the note off her locker door. She looked at the notation and decoded the message.

**H$_2$O 4A 9 I I! –AJ:(**

Missy quickly translated: AJ has an emergency, and she's not happy. Meet by the water fountain near the Discovery Lab (which took up rooms 4A, 4B and 4C).

Missy was experienced with AJ's emergencies. They ranged from what Missy thought of as truly urgent, like forgetting a homework assignment or to study for a quiz, to the frivolous such as needing to share news about a friend or an upcoming event, to a fashion *faux pas* like leaving the house dressed for the wrong day. Whatever the crisis, as AJ's best friend, Missy always tried to help. Last year, Missy managed to tutor AJ on a whole math chapter in the ten minutes before class began; and just last week, she had swapped sweaters and one sock with AJ and managed to improve both their looks. Whatever the crisis, AJ and Missy could find a workable solution together.

When Missy arrived at the water fountain, AJ was surrounded by a swarm including Morgan, Mahdavi, Danny and Kate. Missy calculated the severity of the crisis based on the number of people being consulted. *Five heads to solve one problem.* This must be really serious, Missy thought.

As Missy approached the huddle, AJ's head popped up. AJ was the tallest girl in the sixth grade. As a soccer player and runner, she was lean but not willowy, with a mop of long, red curly hair that she tamed back with headbands and elastics in elaborate configurations.

"You're here!" AJ reached out her arm and pulled Missy into the huddle. "Great! We need you!"

Missy was relieved to see AJ had remembered #FITSD. AJ's rhinestone-studded neon shades sat upon her head like a princess crown and matched her bejeweled ballet flats perfectly. "Hey guys," Missy whispered, greeting the others. "AJ, what's the crisis?"

AJ beamed, "You cracked my message?"

"I did. What's going on?" Missy asked.

AJ peeked above the huddle and scanned the hall before speaking. Then she ducked down and in a hushed voice she started her story, "I was just telling the girls and Danny . . ." AJ's voice trailed off, as a teacher approached the water fountain and took a sip.

"You won't believe it! The fashion club has its first competition in a mere two weeks!"

The crowd gasped.

"Shucks!" Danny said. Missy noticed that Danny had embraced #FITSD too. He wore aviator sun glasses and had somehow painted the tip of his nose white, which made Missy smile.

"Seriously?!" Kate interjected. In her crouched position, Missy could not see the whole of her outfit, but she knew it would be a replica of the school's old uniform, which had not been enforced since the second grade. "I knew it would be soon, but gosh!" Kate said.

"We have to get organized! I'll die if we fail!" AJ said dramatically.

"How can we possibly get our looks together so quickly?" Morgan asked. Morgan was dressed neatly, as was her usual style. Like Kate, Morgan wore a tan skirt and a blue golf shirt, but Morgan's nod to #FITSD was a small sunburst pin attached to the collar of her white cardigan.

"OMG! Can we make it work?" Mahdavi asked.

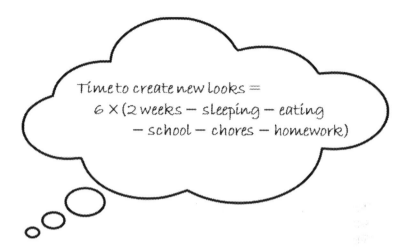

Missy looked at the faces of the people huddled around; each was stunned silent. Her mind was spinning as she calculated the number of days and hours of free time they each would have between now and the competition.

"We've got time!" Missy shouted arriving at her conclusion. Missy startled the others and caught the eye of Mrs. Towers, the gym teacher, heading down the hallway toward them.

"Eight minutes until the bell, kids," Mrs. Towers said tapping her watch as she passed by them. Mrs. Towers always wore workout gear in school. Every day she wore the same uniform of a gray t-shirt sporting the CHAPS Knights team logo with black running pants and black trainers. She kept her long, blond hair pulled back into a low ponytail. Missy imagined Mrs. Towers, who stood at least six feet tall and was rail thin, could have been a beautiful fashion model with her hair and make-up done up and wearing the right clothes.

Doesn't she get bored wearing the same dull clothes every day? Missy wondered to herself, as she watched Mrs. Towers turn the corner. Then Missy ducked her head back into the huddle.

"Really? You think we can get enough work done in such a short time," AJ whispered to Missy.

Morgan spoke up, "Well, at least we have some weekends. I bet we can put something together in time."

They all nodded, regaining their confidence. Missy also reassured the group, "By my calculations, we've got plenty of time!"

"Our first official fashion club meeting is Monday," Kate said, "but I'm sure we can make a plan and work over the weekend to be ready by the competition."

"Okay," Missy said. "Look at us!" Missy spun around and then pointed to Danny's shades and Mahdavi's colorful scarf. Danny snapped his fingers in a zee configuration to reinforce Missy's statement. "We are Fashion Forward —all the way!" Missy said and high-fived with AJ, then Danny.

"Okay! AJ said, relieved her crisis had been managed. "Let's meet in the cafeteria at lunchtime and figure out what we need to do next."

"Great!" Missy and Morgan said in unison. "JINX!" they both sang out just as the bell rang.

*Eleven-forty-eight. Twelve minutes to the lunch bell,* Missy calculated. The morning seemed to drag on. Even while Ms. Jameson taught a lesson on calculating ratios, one of Missy's favorite topics, Missy found it hard to concentrate. Her mind kept drifting to visions of the fashion club's first fashion competition. She pictured Ms. Jameson wearing a high-tech gown that lit up when she walked and gestured toward the whiteboard. Ms. Jameson was generally all buttoned-up, preferring to wear dark colored pantsuits or skirts and coordinating blouses. Ms. Jameson was anything but flashy.

"Missy?" Ms. Jameson called on her. "Missy, can you answer?"

"Uh. What?" Missy said startled. "I mean, excuse me. I didn't follow the question."

Ms. Jameson raised one eyebrow at Missy, and then called on an eager James Kim to answer the question. "The answer is one-twenty-fourth," said James confidently sneering at Missy.

"Of course it is," Missy scolded herself under her breath for not paying attention. She wrote out the equation in her math notebook. She listened closely as Ms. Jameson dictated the class's homework, then carefully packed up her planner and notebook just as the lunch bell rang.

When Missy stood up to leave, Ms. Jameson motioned for Missy to come to her desk. Missy thought for sure she was about to get a lecture on daydreaming in class. Instead, Ms. Jameson said, "I hope you're planning to come to the math club meeting after school on Monday, Missy! We could really use your skills on the team."

"Oh," Missy said, "I'm still thinking about it." Missy didn't want to disappoint Ms. Jameson, but there was no way she would be joining math club. Missy was certain that would permanently tag her as a super geek. Missy fidgeted with her pack, said goodbye and slipped out of the room.

She scrambled through the crowded hallway dodging people making their way back to their lockers in order to get to the cafeteria as quickly as she could without breaking the school's no-running-in-the-halls rule. The more she thought about it, the happier she was. Math club would be impossible to attend because she committed to the fashion club and they met at the same time. That was her out—a scheduling conflict! Missy was relieved that she now had a great excuse.

When she arrived, the line for hot lunch at the cafeteria counter already wound its way back and around the turnstile. So Missy opted for a cold lunch and picked up a pre-made sandwich and a bag of fruit crisps. She swiped her cafeteria card at the register and headed toward the table where she could see the others were already gathering.

Morgan caught up to her and touched her arm to get her attention. "Hey, Miss! I was just talking to Ms. Jameson. I think I'm going to go to the math club meeting on Monday, and split my time so I can also go to the fashion club meeting. You wanna join me?"

"What?" Missy asked. "Uh. No. I don't think so," she stammered suddenly feeling panicked that her great excuse might not be so great after all.

The girls made their way around the maze of cafeteria tables and settled at the one that Danny had reserved with his backpack, both of his shoes and his sweatshirt. Missy and Morgan sat on the long bench opposite Danny, AJ and Mahdavi who were already seated at the table. Missy pinched her nose and picked up one of Danny's shoes by the laces. She passed it across the table to him. "Thanks for saving us seats," she said in a nasally voice.

"Sure thang, y'all. It was my pleasure," Danny said with a southern accent that always made Missy smile. Danny started at CHAPS in sixth grade. His family had moved from South Carolina where he had been home-schooled. He was tall for his age with a mop of dark brown hair cut fashionably floppy, copying all the current teen icons. He had tested up a year. So, even though he was barely eleven, Danny had been placed into sixth grade. Danny seemed to love CHAPS and all his classes. Missy liked how he wanted to meet everyone and try everything. When Missy had asked Danny about his accent, he exclaimed, "That's no accent. That's just southern charm."

AJ started speed-talking, which she did whenever she was excited. Missy could tell that no one was following her.

"AJ. AJ," Missy spoke up. "Slow down. Let's go back to the beginning."

AJ took a breath and started speaking normally again. "Okay. This is what we know," AJ glanced at her smartphone hidden on her lap under the table where she had input her intel, "We have exactly ten and one-half days to get organized and design and create three to five separate looks." As she spoke, AJ's words sped up and merged together. Missy gave her a slow-down signal with her hands.

"Right," said Morgan. "And the competition category is 'True to You' according to Mrs. Frisch, our fashion club mentor who happens to be my homeroom teacher."

Kate slid onto the bench, knocking off Danny's remaining shoe. She used her foot to push it across the floor to Danny's side of the table. "I found out that we can work as a group or in pairs. I read the rules on the library computer and that was clearly stated."

"That makes a lot of sense," Missy said. "Since there are six of us here, we can work in teams of two, so we will have at least three looks, and maybe more if there are others in the club who we don't know yet."

Danny scratched his head. "Let's pair up then."

AJ grabbed Missy's hand. Kate nodded to Morgan from the end of the table.

"Okay Mahdavi! We've got this, girl," Danny said and flicked the edge of her scarf in the air.

With the teams decided, Danny asked, "I'm just wondering . . . where do we get our supplies? Like material and zippers. You know, buttons and notions and *et ceteras?*"

"OMG!" AJ put her head on the table. "I hadn't even thought of *that!*"

Missy felt a surge of energy that pumped from her toes to her head. "I know!" she shouted pointing at the sign in the cafeteria. It was the twin to the sign she'd seen earlier that morning above the lockers.

AJ raised her head and looked at Missy, "What?!"

They all swiveled in their seats following Missy's gaze to read the sign. Mahdavi giggled. "That's cute, but I don't get it. How does 'er' answer the question?"

"Not 'er,' YOU ARE," Danny said. "Get it? The letters U and R are cut out of the words Reduce and Reuse?"

"Hah!" Mahdavi laughed. "That's hilarious. I guess they want us to recycle more."

"Exactly!" Missy said. "Look at my OOTD." Missy stood up and spun around for the second time that day. "It's completely made up of upcycled clothes! These shorts were my old jeans that got too short for me as pants. This shirt was a plain boring t-shirt. And, I totally customized these kicks," she said standing on one leg and showing off her painted sneakers.

"Wow!" said Danny. "That's a great idea! I bet we all have clothes that don't fit or hand-me-downs that need updating or other items that could just use some PIZZAZZ!"

"You Are right!" said Morgan, exaggerating a wink.

Missy got the joke right away and repeated, "U R—no you are!" and they all laughed.

"I'll have to see," said Kate tentatively, "but maybe ..."

"Perfect!" said AJ. "Problem solved!"

## FASHION HACK

What is upcycling?

Upcycling is a way of turning old and discarded materials into something special, giving the item a new life through your transformation.

## FASHION HACK: T-SHIRT PILLOW HOW-TO

Turn a well-loved tee into a new pillow. Find an old t-shirt that you loved for the color or its graphic but has lost its shape or no longer fits you or has a small stain. Turn it inside-out and draw a square around the area you want to feature on your pillow, then sew along that line, leaving about a four-inch section unsewn. Use that opening to turn the t-shirt inside-right and stuff it with batting or strips of cut up discarded clothing. Sew up the hole then hot glue oversized buttons or other embellishments. And, enjoy your upcycled pillow!

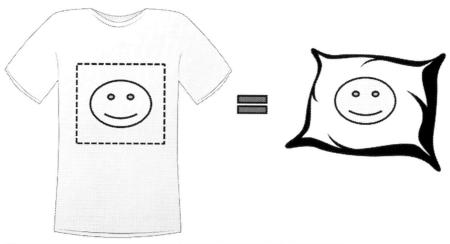

# Figures and Icons

"Settle down. Settle down!" Mrs. Frisch repeated for the third time. The fashion club was having its first official meeting of the year and everyone was excited to talk about designing and how the club worked and to learn more about their first competition of the year.

"Now let's see," Mrs. Frisch started, looking at an index card she held in her perfectly manicured hand. Mrs. Frisch looked amazing, as usual.

For a middle school teacher, Missy thought Mrs. Frisch always looked glamorous and put together. Today, she wore navy cigarette pants, which were all clean lines, narrowing down to the ankle. The pants stopped right at the top of her ankles which peeked out above her bright red, canvas espadrilles. Mrs. Frisch sported a striped navy and white, three-quarters sleeve jersey shirt. To bring the whole look together, she topped it off with a nautical themed blue and red silk scarf with gold anchors on it. *Très chic*, Missy thought, wondering why this outfit made her want to speak French.

*Navy and red plus gold anchors and white equal dy-no-mite.* With her bobbed brown hair and golden highlights, Missy thought Mrs. Frisch might spend her summers acting in movies or posing for magazine covers.

Everyone settled in their seats at the raised draft tables. "First, we need a name for the fashion club," Mrs. Frisch continued. "Second, we need to elect a few leaders. And, third, we need to do some planning."

© Melissa A. Borza and CA 2017
M. A. Borza, *Fashion Figures*, DOI 10.1007/978-1-4842-2274-4_3

AJ's hand shot into the air as she bounced up and down in her seat waiting for Mrs. Frisch to call on her. "Yes, Andrea?" Mrs. Frisch asked.

"What about our first competition?" AJ asked.

"Right. I'm so thrilled to see many of you have taken the initiative to get a head start! We will absolutely get to that!" Mrs. Frisch exclaimed. "Let's get the *administrivia* out of the way—then we'll jump into the fun!"

Everyone agreed to that and started brainstorming possible club names. This led to a heated discussion among all the club members, which included another four students from the seventh and eighth grades whom Missy had never met. They too must have heard the rumors about the upcoming event, as they had brought looks of their own. Missy was eager to hear about their inspiration and design process.

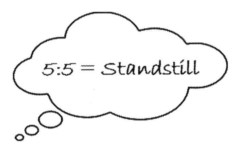

Finally, the students narrowed down their club name choices to two possibilities: Fashion Figures and Fashion Icons. *Five against five is a standstill.* And, when the matter could not be settled by a vote, Mrs. Frisch suggested a compromise taking terms from both name ideas. This new combination suited everyone perfectly and the vote to name their club "Figures and Icons" was unanimous.

"Loooove it!" Danny shouted puckering his face and walking like a model. Everyone laughed.

"Okay, designers. Time to elect our club leaders." Mrs. Frisch explained that every club had special roles to help keep activities organized and to be sure everything was planned appropriately. She also explained that while not everyone could have a leadership role, everyone in the club was responsible for keeping it fun and making it a great experience.

"We need to elect a president to run our meetings and help lead the planning for activities. We also need a communications manager to coordinate our SocialMe page, write announcements, and blog about our competitions, and we need a treasurer to keep track of our fundraising and expenses."

"If you are interested in one of these roles, please step to the front of the classroom." A strange silence crept across the room as everyone considered the leadership roles and gauged their individual interest.

AJ and Missy made their way to the front of the room, stopping to whisper their preferences to Mrs. Frisch. Two eighth graders also stepped up. After a few minutes, there were still just four people standing with Mrs. Frisch at the head of the class, and the chatter resumed.

"Ahem!" Mrs. Frisch cleared her throat to get everyone's attention. "It seems we have an unusual situation. We have two candidates interested in being president and two candidates interested in being communications manager. We still need a treasurer, which is a vital role for the fashion club! Who's interested in that role? Come on up!"

"I'm terrible at math," said Mahdavi.

"You are not," Morgan insisted. Morgan had slipped into the meeting midway into the voting for the club.

Kate crossed her arms and scowled at Mahdavi's comment, "You could be treasurer, if you wanted."

Danny whispered to Morgan, "My mama says I'm only good at spending money. Not keeping track of it."

AJ elbowed Missy who was standing beside her at the front of the room. "You should be treasurer. You're so great at math. And you love it," she whispered, covering her mouth with her hand.

Missy felt the heat rise up from her stomach to her head, and her cheeks turned bright red. The last thing she wanted to be known for were her math skills. "No way," she whispered. "I'm running for president."

Morgan raised her hand tentatively. "Um. Mrs. Frisch, I suppose I could give it a try. I've never been a treasurer before. It might be fun?" She said the last part like a question, and Mrs. Frisch winked at her.

"Excellent! Yes, it will be fun," Mrs. Frisch reassured her, as she motioned for Morgan to come to the front of the classroom. "Congratulations, Morgan! Come on up. You are the club's treasurer." The students applauded, eager to finish the elections and move on to hear the details of the looming first competition.

Mrs. Frisch turned to the four other candidates standing with her. She spoke briefly to them, then she separated them into two groups. She announced, "Your candidates for president are Paula Teehan and Melissa Maker. Your candidates for communications manager are Andrea Jane Dupre and Yooni Park." AJ tensed up and wrinkled her nose at the use of her full and proper name. It always sounded so strange to her ears.

"Each person will speak for two minutes to share their qualifications for the roles, and then we will vote!" Mrs. Frisch concluded.

Paula Teehan had been the club's communications manager the year before, and she talked about her experience in the club and how she could lead Figures and Icons as club president this school year. Missy spoke about her love of fashion and her eagerness to help the club do well. In the end, Paula won by a single vote—Missy's. Missy respected her experience and hoped that she could work closely with Paula and learn how to be a good leader. In the second vote, AJ won the communications manager position, as she was already well known for her social media skills and daily SocialMe postings, which had a tremendous following.

With the elections wrapped up and only a few minutes left in the meeting, Mrs. Frisch talked about the competitions ahead and how they would work. Each competition would have a theme to inspire original designs, and for most events, teams would show three to five looks, which meant that the club had to work as a team most of the time and not as individuals. There would be events later in the year where each participant could show their own designs, but that would come later. Each club was responsible for getting their own fabrics, notions, and supplies, though they could solicit donations from local businesses. Mrs. Frisch brought out the club's stash—club leftovers and donations from previous years. To Missy's eyes, it was a magic box, filled with mystery and potential. Mrs. Frisch continued to share that they would act as their own models. They would decide who would wear the looks for each competition so the models could be fitted properly. Everyone buzzed and shared their excitement.

"Finally," Mrs. Frisch said, "next week we have our first competition. I see several of you have brought in designs. Work among yourselves to sort out who will model them and in our remaining time let's work on fittings."

They chose AJ, Kate, Mahdavi, a seventh grader named SallyAnn, and Yooni as models for the first competition. The girls quickly changed into the outfits, and Mrs. Frisch consulted on simple adjustments and fitting techniques to consider. She reminded them that accessories and finishing touches like shoes and jewelry and handbags would complete their looks. Everyone left the meeting excited and feeling ready for their first event.

The bus ride from CHAPS to New Milford Regional seemed to take forever. Seven miles never seemed so long as when a whole busload of students was eager to arrive. *Thirty miles per hour means we should arrive in fourteen minutes plus stop lights plus loading and unloading.* Will we ever get there, Missy wondered.

When they finally arrived, Mrs. Frisch, a few CHAPS teachers, and all ten members of Figures and Icons de-boarded. The club members carried vinyl zippered garment bags, make-up cases and boxes with shoes and other accessories. Mrs. Frisch pulled a large rolling suitcase behind her. It was the club's show go-box, which held scissors, double-sided tape, a travel steam iron, needles, threads, buttons, zippers and a complete first aid kit.

Today, Mrs. Frisch had really outdone herself! She was dressed in a royal blue sheath dress and a smart cropped jacket that matched the dress perfectly. Her black heels click-click-clicked as she walked ahead of the students. Everyone marched in a line behind Mrs. Frisch. She led the students into the school and down a side hallway to the gym.

"Spectators proceed to the gymnasium bleachers. Figures and Icons, we are heading into the locker room. There are six teams competing today! We will share our locker room with two other teams. Please be courteous and respectful of our hosts and other competitors," Mrs. Frisch reminded the students.

As she entered and looked around, Missy was confused. The locker room had been transformed. She never would have guessed that sports teams spent any time in here. Pipes with drapes hung along one side of the room creating individual nooks to give models some privacy while they changed clothes. Three raised platforms, several full-length mirrors and three clothing racks on wheels had been placed strategically around the room so that each team had a defined working area. As Figures and Icons set up in their designated space, students from the competing schools came by and introduced themselves. Everyone was nervous and excited. As the students began opening their garment bags, a hush came over the room. Teams concentrated on dressing their models and preparing them for the runway show.

Missy squeezed AJ's hand. She carefully removed their dress from its garment bag. Missy and AJ had designed the dress and then constructed it using material from Molly's high school prom dress, an old t-shirt from Mr. Maker, and a few neckties that AJ's step-dad had contributed to the cause. It could have been a hot mess, but they kept it simple and tasteful while trying to reflect their personalities.

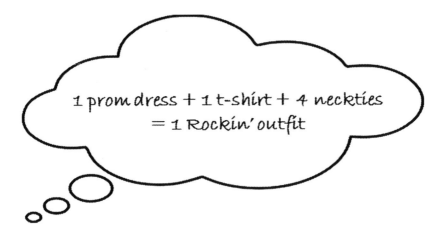

$$1 \text{ prom dress} + 1 \text{ t-shirt} + 4 \text{ neckties} = 1 \text{ Rockin' outfit}$$

Missy had wanted the dress to be knee-length and AJ wanted it to be flowy, so they combined their visions and they loved their final creation. After two summers at her favorite maker camp, Camp Winnebago, where Missy took classes in machine sewing, Missy was an expert seamstress. Plus, G-ma had taught her a few hand sewing techniques for embellishment.

Everything Missy loved was coming together. The two-piece look she created with AJ combined black lace over a sleeveless, white jersey crop top with a printed black and white floral skirt with deep side pockets that poofed out. A textured black silk tie made up the waistline and tied at the side. The outfit shimmered when it moved under the fluorescent light in the locker room. It was sure to dazzle on the runway.

"Not bad for one weekend of work!" AJ bragged.

Missy nodded as she smoothed the lace with her hands. "Twelve hours, thirty-nine minutes, to be exact," she said. "Now let's put it on you!"

AJ carefully took the dress into one of the changing stalls to put on, while Missy unpacked five bracelets and two necklaces, two handbags, three pairs of black and one pair of nude shoes. They had not decided how they would accessorize or which shoes to wear, so AJ had packed all of her dress shoes and Missy had borrowed some jewelry from G-ma and a few bags to try.

When AJ stepped up on the platform in the dress, Mrs. Frisch stepped over. "Andrea, you look wonderful! Let's get your hair up and put on a little blush." She waved over Morgan who carried a small case that looked like a fishing tackle box and wore an apron holding multiple brushes and hair notions. Though she was not a model for this show, Morgan was made up, dressed in a stylish one-piece romper with frilly shorts, and she looked ready to walk the runway. "Can you help AJ with a touch of make-up?" Mrs. Frisch directed.

Morgan worked quickly, pinning up AJ's curly red hair, leaving a few curls to frame her face, and swooped and swirled a brushful of blush on each cheek. "There you are," Morgan said and flounced over to Kate who was just coming out of a changing stall.

Missy was amazed that Morgan could work so well and so quickly, especially as AJ was up and down trying on each of the shoes and teetering around on the platform. They settled on the nude shoes and added all the jewelry Missy had borrowed. They decided to skip a bag.

"I love it!" Missy declared and snapped a photo of AJ alone on the platform and another one posing with her. Then she posted them both with the hashtag TrueToYou.

The whole team scuttled silently between the clothing racks, go-bags, boxes, changing rooms and shared platform. It was like a choreographed dance; everyone somehow knew what to do. Whenever anyone needed help, someone appeared with the solution. Missy felt so grown up and proud to be showing off something she had designed and made with her very own hands!

"Okay. Two minutes to the runway models. Take your numbers as you exit and hold onto them. Everyone else, head out to chairs and bleachers," Mrs. Frisch announced. "We'll line up by the door and I'll send the models out one at a time. Remember to smile and hold up your number for the judges to see."

Figures and Icons was the first team to walk the runway. Danny sat next to Missy and commented on each outfit as the models showed them off. It was hard to hear him over the soundtrack playing over the loudspeaker. When his design partner, Mahdavi, emerged Danny nearly leapt out of his seat. "Hot dog!" he said. "She looks great!"

Mahdavi wore an outfit that looked like a sari shrunk to just above her knees. Layers of colorful fabric swayed around her as she walked. She winked at her teammates at the end of the runway, tossed her head back throwing her long, flowing brown hair over her shoulder, then quickly turned and walked back to the locker room.

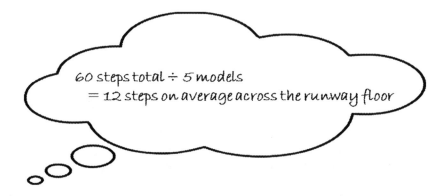

60 steps total ÷ 5 models
= 12 steps on average across the runway floor

Missy nodded. Everyone looked like a real model. She counted the steps each model took from the time she stepped out onto the runway until she turned to go back. She divided that number by the five models on her team. *Twelve steps on average from door across floor.*

When the Figures and Icons models finished on the runway, they came out and sat in another section of the gym opposite Missy and Danny. Missy was disappointed that AJ could not be next to her for the rest of the show. She waved across the runway and AJ waved back with her paddle number, "134." Then they quickly became mesmerized by the remaining competition.

The schools' few spectators whooped and whistled for their schools' teams. In awe of the outfits marching down the runway, Missy's mouth hung open.

"You catchin' flies?" Danny asked Missy. He tapped Missy's chin with his index finger, and she closed her mouth.

"I'm so impressed," Missy said.

"And inspired," she heard Paula say from right behind her. "Isn't it great how everything comes together out of the chaos? I just love it!"

Missy and Danny nodded in agreement. This experience was so different from anything she had ever done before. Even at maker camp, though they had a show at the end of the two weeks of camp, the production did not measure up to this, plus the fashion was intermingled with so many of the campers' other creations.

"Just wait till we get to state finals," said SallyAnn enthusiastically. A normally reserved and very quiet seventh grader in the club, SallyAnn wore a gray

CHAPS sweatshirt over her OOTD. Her skin was very pale, and she had delicate features. With the shirt pulled down over her knees, SallyAnn looked as if the sweatshirt had swallowed her whole, Missy thought.

"Don't get ahead of yourself," Paula cautioned. "This is our first runway of the year. We've got a long, LONG way to go before we can even talk about that!"

Missy hit herself on the head with the butt of her hand. OMG, she thought. She had been so wrapped up in the production, she had forgotten to take any photos. She pulled out her smartphone and snapped pictures of the remaining looks, adding notes to remember how the outfits made her feel.

The music suddenly changed, and the remaining models took their seats. Missy leaned right and posed next to Danny for a selfie and then leaned left and posed with Morgan. As she reviewed the photos, she saw Paula had photo-bombed them both. Missy laughed and posted her pix with the TrueToYou hashtag.

The six school club advisors and another adult marched in a line to the end of the stage. Missy turned her attention back to the runway as the music quieted.

"Welcome, students and spectators. I am principal of New Milford Regional. We are so happy to host the first fashion club meet of the season. Congratulations to our teams for an amazing show. Let's hear it for the fashion club teams." The crowd applauded and whistled. For a small group, their squeals and cheers made it feel as if the gym was packed full. The students in the bleachers stomped their feet and shook the whole room.

"Yes! Yes!" Principal Edwards spoke over the crowd, and used his hands to mime, "Quiet down. Now I'm sure you are all eager to hear the results, but first let's introduce the schools and their advisors."

Missy tuned out a bit and looked around the room. She tried to spot G-ma or her father among the spectators. She knew her dad had to work, but G-ma promised to be there. And, there she was sitting in the bleachers. G-ma waved wildly when she noticed Missy looking in her direction, and Missy waved back, smiling.

Each advisor spent a few minutes introducing their school and having their teams stand up to be recognized. Then came the introduction of the judges, which included the owner of a local fabric store called Notions, Mrs. Kilpatrick, the art and design teacher at New Milford Regional, Mrs. Lopez, and finally a special guest judge, the real-life model and designer Sarah DeMott. They all waved from their seats at the end of the runway.

The audience cheered. Missy was practically dumbstruck to see Sarah DeMott. Here they were in a small New Jersey town and the world-famous, actual cover girl, Sarah DeMott, was judging their fashion meet. She had to pinch herself to be sure she wasn't dreaming. "Ouch," Missy said, reminding her that this was no dream.

"We'll announce the winners by their numbers, so they can come up on the runway to hear critiques and feedback from our judges. If you designed in teams, the whole team should come up," the principal explained as the team advisors stepped down from the runway. "As a reminder, advisors will receive written critiques for all looks to share with their teams." He took an envelope from a student at the end of the runway. "Okay. Here we go," he announced. "We have number one-oh-nine. One-zero-nine. Designers and models, come on up."

Everyone scanned the model section as no one seemed to be moving. Then, one teammate from New Milford Regional elbowed her friend who had set her number on the floor. She popped up with a screech and ran to the runway. From Missy's section, two students got up to join the model. The three of them danced in a circle on the runway.

"Okay. Next, we have one-thirty-four. One-three-four," the principal read.

Missy didn't hesitate, she was out of her seat and up on the stage before AJ could get there. They hugged each other tightly jumping up and down.

The principal paused, turned to smile at the group on stage then said, "And, finally, please join us on the stage, number one-eighteen. One-one-eight!"

A loud whistle emanated from the crowd and someone shouted, "Go IVY!"

"Judges, teachers, students and spectators, I present the winners of the True To You fashion competition," the principal said gesturing toward the group that had gathered on the runway behind him.

Everyone clapped and cheered, while Mrs. Frisch and another advisor came out and organized the teams on the stage at the top of the runway, so they could be seen by everyone.

When the crowd settled down, the principal left the stage and handed his microphone to the judges seated at the head of the runway. Mrs. Kilpatrick spoke first, "Let me start by saying that you are all winners. Each look we saw on the runway wowed us. I am so knocked out by what you have accomplished at your age. We judges had a tough time picking only three finalists."

Missy fidgeted with her ponytail. She tugged it upward, imagining it was shooting to the moon. AJ touched her arm and Missy brought it down from her head back down to her side.

AJ whispered. "I totally cannot believe we are here. This is awesome." AJ swayed slightly, shifting her weight from foot to foot.

"Before we make our final selections, we would like to hear from each team about your inspiration and about how your look reflects the True To You theme," Mrs. Kilpatrick continued.

The same student who had delivered the envelope to the principal, appeared on the stage with three hand-held microphones. He showed each team where the "on" switch was and then disappeared.

"Let's start with one-eighteen," supermodel designer Sarah DeMott said. "Tell us the name of your school, your team and share your inspiration."

Ivy fumbled with her microphone, so Missy reached over and helped her switch it on.

"Oh. Got it. My name is Ivy," she started. "I go to Fairmount Prep and our team is called the Fashionanimas." She paused as her team stood up and cheered.

Ivy was wearing an all-white minidress with a backless halter top that showed off her shoulders. It was belted by a funky sculpture made of black paper clips intertwined with red paracord. Missy had never seen anything like this dress and she was fascinated by the fabric draping that seemed so effortless.

"Uh. It's my design, and I am modeling too," Ivy said. "My inspiration came to me as I was thinking about who was my muse—and I started thinking about mythology and the Greek and Roman goddesses—I thought, 'How can I turn that into something that reflects my personality?' and this is what I came up with?" Ivy ended her statement like a question, which always caught Missy off guard. She had been drilled by G-ma and her father specifically not to do that, because it sounds like you don't believe what you are saying. So, she tried hard not to speak in questions when she was making statements.

Sarah DeMott said, "Well, I just love it. I would wear this on the red carpet. Tell me more about your belt. That's so unusual and interesting."

Ivy thought for a moment and then spoke, "Actually, engineering is my first love. I love to put things together in interesting ways and I was playing around with some paper clips and before I knew it, I had a whole chain of them and I asked myself what more could I do to make that chain functional."

Missy was stunned. She had never thought of using something like a paperclip in her fashions before. She wondered what other office supplies and trinkets she could make use of in some innovative way.

"Thank you, Ivy," said Mrs. Lopez. "I think you did a great job, too. Let's hear from one-thirty-four, next."

AJ grasped Missy's hand and squeezed hard. Missy used her thumb to switch on the microphone. "Hi, I'm Missy Maker," she passed the microphone to AJ, "And I'm AJ Dupre. We're from Cherry Hill."

AJ passed the microphone back to Missy. "Our team is Figures and Icons," she said and her schoolmates and team answered with whoops and chants of "Go CHAPS! Go CHAPS!"

"We were inspired by our school's recycling campaign," Missy said. She heard a loud whistle and looked up. G-ma was standing in the bleachers smiling widely. Missy continued, "We loved the idea of taking something old and remaking it into something completely new. Plus, our club got a late start this year and we had no money for materials," she said and the audience laughed.

"I enjoyed the mixture of textures and patterns," Sarah DeMott commented.

"I really liked the styling," Mrs. Kilpatrick added.

"Yes." The art teacher judge, Mrs. Lopez agreed, "This look is so modern and funky."

AJ's excitement overwhelmed her. Her sway became a full-on hop from one foot to the other. Missy shook her hand and arm and AJ slowed her jig back into a slow and steady sway.

"Good job. Okay. Team one-zero-nine, there are so many of you," Mrs. Kilpatrick announced.

The last team was huddled together, with their model in the middle holding the microphone. "We're the Gazingers from St. Mark's Academy. I'm Amy," said the model. "I'm Anthony," Anthony said dipping his head to the microphone. "And I am Lola."

Amy wore a two-piece outfit. The top was a blue square, which, to Missy, looked like a pillowcase with a head hole and arm holes cut out of it. The blue top was layered over a long pencil skirt that stayed narrow all the way to the floor. Missy wondered how Amy had walked down the runway without tripping on the dress.

Amy held the microphone while Lola continued, "We were inspired by sewing simplicity. We wanted to make a look using only straight lines and only sewing where it was absolutely needed. So you can see we have raw edges and really only one nearly continuous seam in each garment. We think it's True To You because we each added one element to the project while keeping the simplicity and straight line idea at the center."

"That's so cool," Sarah DeMott said.

"I agree," said Mrs. Lopez. "That's really a unique perspective!"

Mrs. Kilpatrick wrapped up, "Yes. I love your concept, though that skirt could probably be executed a little better so your model can get around more easily."

After the teams' remarks, the principal hopped up on the runway. "Let's hear it for our finalists one more time." The cheers and stomping came up and quickly died down as everyone was eager to hear the results.

The envelope boy appeared again passing a new envelope on. The principal pulled out a card and read from it. In third place, Gazingers!" St. Mark's

Academy fashion club advisor came up on the stage with a small trophy. The designers each held a part of it and posed for a picture.

Missy and AJ and Ivy were shaking with excitement and holding hands.

"In first place in the True to You event is Fashionanimas!"

Missy's stomach dropped and she thought she would cry right on the spot. AJ pulled her in and gave her a hug. Then AJ cheered. "Great job, Ivy!" Missy liked that about AJ. She guessed it was AJ's good-sportsman's nature from all her years as an athlete that taught her to always cheer on the winner even in the face of defeat.

Mrs. Frisch joined them on stage carrying the second-place trophy. She held it high in the air as the team joined in and gathered close for a photo. That professional photo was followed by a series of selfies that were texted far and wide to social networks and beyond.

The Fairmount Prep advisor hopped onto the runway with a huge trophy. Ivy posed with her advisor, and that completed the event.

The competitors all headed back to the locker room to change into their normal clothes and to pack up for the bus ride back to CHAPS. Missy followed her teammates back to the locker room. She focused on cleaning up their area, picking up bobby pins, socks and random notions to pack away or throw away, the whole time calculating probabilities, wondering what she could have done differently to bring home the first-place trophy.

## MATH HACK: WHAT IS A PROBABILITY?

Statistics is an area of math that focuses on probability. A probability is the likelihood of something occurring. It can be calculated using a ratio between all possibilities and likely occurrences. It is often represented as a fraction or as a percent. Percent means per one hundred.

Here's a hack for you: Figure out the probability of getting a blue gumball from a jar of 30 gumballs where there are 10 each of red, blue and yellow gumballs. Looking at the whole jar, you know that 10 out of 30 will be blue gumballs. So, your chance of getting a blue one is 10/30 or 1/3. The probability is 1 in 3 chances or 33% that you will receive a blue gumball.

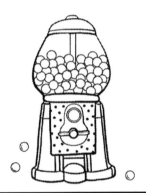

## FUN FACT

Weather newscasters use probabilities to report on the weather. There is no way to know exactly what the weather will be on any given day, so they use trends and data to determine the most likely scenarios.

# Divided We Stand

The bus ride back to school seemed to take twice as long as it had taken to get to the competition. Spectators and club members kept up the chatter on the bus, while Missy counted telephone poles along the route and tried not to think about why she felt sad. After all, this was her first ever real fashion competition, and her team had placed among the top contestants. She guessed that was pretty good for a look they had put together in a weekend, using recycled materials.

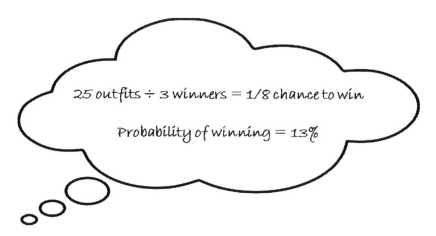

25 outfits ÷ 3 winners = 1/8 chance to win

Probability of winning = 13%

Missy scrolled through the pictures on her phone. *Twenty-five outfits and only three winners.* Missy calculated the odds of getting any awards facing that level of competition. The probability was lower than Missy expected—only about 13%.

She took out her phone and looked at all the pix from the event. One selfie had her and AJ with their heads together making goofy eyes into the camera. Suddenly Missy remembered that in the sweeping excitement of the event, she completely flaked and forgot to capture all the CHAPS looks. She would have to talk to her friends to see if anyone else had thought to take pictures of the CHAPS outfits. Missy hoped at least one person had the presence of mind to capture it all. Luckily, she had taken photos of the remaining competitors.

The notes she wrote in her phone brought her back to each exciting and lovely moment of the show. She felt so many emotions just thinking back to the hours she had just lived through. Camp Winnebago had had a Maker Fair at the conclusion of her summer camp. That had been fun too. The Fair included a kind of show where every camper shared and showed off what they made during the camp. Missy had sported the blue spandex shorts she had sewn along with an oversized tie-dyed tee she had made in shades of blues and purples. Missy looked down at her hands remembering how long it had taken to get all the dye off of them. G-ma and Mr. Maker showered her with compliments and Missy ended up making her dad a matching tie-dye shirt that he wore with his pajama bottoms. Missy didn't remember having these wild feelings of excitement and anxiety.

As she continued scrolling through the photos, Missy remembered one look that she had expected to be a finalist but that had not won any recognition. The look appeared to be a long denim dress, but when the model walked, Missy could see that the outfit was a wide-legged jumpsuit. The blue denim apron covered the model's top half like a fitted tube with armholes. The jumpsuit had deep side pockets, which Missy thought had looked so cool. Missy also liked a simple tank top and shorts outfit she saw. Then she came upon another favorite—and remembered Ivy and her architectural approach to fashion. Missy daydreamed while the others chattered away.

Seated next to Missy on the bus, AJ was bobbing up and down in her seat talking excitedly with the other Figures and Icons members. "That was WILD. I was never so excited and nervous and happy all at once in my whole life! Not even when I crossed the 5K finish line first last spring! I feel so . . .," AJ looked up to the ceiling trying to come up with the right word, "accomplished!" AJ was talking a mile a minute and with her constant bouncing, Missy feared AJ might fly right down the aisle of the bus if the driver had to stop fast. Thankfully, everyone, including AJ, had their seat belts on.

"I know exactly what you mean," Danny declared. "That was so fun and everyone looked awesome and it was all so, I-don't-know, professional. Just like we are real designers and real models."

"We are!" Paula said. "We are real designers. We created new ideas and we sewed fabrics together to make those ideas into actual clothing. Then we dressed up our very own models and sent them down an actual runway. We are real designers and real models."

On an inhale, Mahdavi all but screamed. "It's totally just dawned on me. We are!" She side-hugged Danny who was in the seat beside her. "We ARE! Oh, my goodness!" Danny and Mahdavi put their heads together and giggled, chanting, "We are real designers. We are real designers." Soon, the whole bus caught on and everyone repeated the mantra.

Missy understood exactly what they meant. She and AJ had worked together to create something real that started from a few sketches on Missy's math notebook. Then, what started out on paper was brought to life. They pieced together random materials until they finally finished. Who else could have imagined putting a man's tie and a t-shirt together with a lace gown to create such a magical look as Missy and AJ had done?

Missy thought back to the Aha! moment in her bedroom. They had sketches strewn all over the floor and articles of clothing and donated notions and fabrics covering Missy's desk and bed. Pi pranced around as if inspecting each piece. With his tail in the air he had checked their work over finally settling himself on the sketch Missy and AJ had chosen to bring to life. That moment, when it all came together, thrilled Missy.

Oddly enough, that moment reminded Missy of when she learned how to do long division. The actual second when everything just clicked and she understood. "Hmm," Missy said, smiling to herself. She loved connecting the dots in her life, finding and creating patterns. And, she had just realized a whole new world of discovery lay ahead for her.

When the bus arrived back at CHAPS, Mrs. Frisch gathered the club members in a circle on the school's front lawn before dismissing them to go home. "I'm so proud of all of you! You should all feel great about this competition. Not everyone can take home a prize, and the judges were clearly impressed." Mrs. Frisch looked around the circle. Most of the fashion club members had their arms around each other's shoulders listening intently to their mentor. "At our next meeting, we'll take a look at the judges' comments. We can always learn by keeping our minds and hearts open! Let's have a cheer before you all rush off to get home."

The fashion club members piled their hands on top of Mrs. Frisch's in the center of the circle, then Paula led them in a cheer. "CHAPS designs are A-OK! Figures and Icons all the waaaaaaaaaay!"

Everyone shouted, "GOOOO CHAPS!"

As the circle opened up and began to disband, Danny said to the models, "You girls did a great job! You really showed off the designs!" He clapped his hands and jumped up, "And, I can't believe we won!"

"We didn't win," Missy corrected. "We came in second."

"Huh?" Danny said, confused. "There were a lot of teams that did not make it back up on that stage, Missy. With a second-place trophy, we surely did win! The judges loved the design you and AJ came up with!" Everyone nodded their agreement and Missy smiled back.

Danny patted Missy's arm.

"You're right, Danny. Sorry I said that," Missy said sheepishly.

"What a day!" he said and turned to hug Mahdavi who had stepped up beside him. "I've got some new ideas, Mad. Can't wait to show you my sketches!" Danny linked arms with Mahdavi as they walked toward the parking lot where their parents waited to pick them up.

"Great job, everyone," Mrs. Frisch repeated as she packed up and checked her bag.

"I can't wait to read all the judges' comments and feedback," Yooni interjected. "I really want to know what they liked and how we can improve."

"Me too," said Morgan. "I'm excited for another competition." The others repeated similar comments and exchanged hugs. They scanned the school parking lot, looking for their parents and siblings who were coming to pick them up.

Missy and AJ were the last two left waiting, so they plopped down on the grass. Mrs. Frisch had recruited two senior boys coming off the football field to carry the go-bag and the boxes with the garments folded in them back to the studio.

AJ plucked at the grass between them. "Hey Miss?" she asked.

"Yes?" Missy asked in response, looking after the boys and Mrs. Frisch heading back into the building.

AJ waited for Missy to look at her, then she spoke: "That was really cool today. Ya know?"

"I agree," Missy said, "but I was kind of sad for a second. You know? We didn't come in first place." Missy paused and picked out a dandelion from the lawn. "Then I started thinking about the work we did to get there. How everything we did came together to make something really beautiful. We both had different ideas, but then it all worked. And, that's the best part. That's what I loved—working with my best friend. Making something amazing. Together. I can't wait to do it again! You know?"

"Totally," AJ said. "I get it. Coming in the top three was a total rush for me."

"I know," Missy said, "that was cool, too." Missy stood up and brushed the grass from her bottom. AJ followed suit. G-ma had just pulled into the parking lot.

"Let's go," Missy said. They picked up their backpacks along with the bag of shoes and accessories and headed to the car.

## MATH HACK: PERCENTAGES

Calculating percentages can be tricky! Here are some things to know about percentages.

The word percent actually means per, or how many, in one hundred. So, a percentage is a number expressed as a fraction or a ratio of 100. It is denoted using the percent sign, %. Percentages are used to compare numbers or to determine the relative size or quantities of two or more things.

For example, fifteen percent (15%) is equal to 15/100, or 3/20, or 0.15.

Your math grade is a percentage: An A+ means the average of your classwork and test scores is between 98% and 100%, while a C+ is between 77% and 79%.

# Patterns and Problems

Painted blue in Missy's favorite shade: not baby blue, not light blue, but cornflower blue. Missy's room was her sanctuary. She could escape there and be alone or invite friends over to play or spread her things all around to work. Missy's room was larger than most of her friends' bedrooms, because for ten years, she had shared it with her sister Molly. Now that Molly lived in an apartment in her college town, Missy had the room to herself. Her sister had taken her own double bed and dresser for her new bedroom, and Missy now had all the space to herself. That space included everything Missy could ever need: books and bookshelves, a desk and laptop computer, a sewing machine and table, her very own dress form, a walk-in closet—big enough even to fit a bean bag chair, which was the envy of all her friends, and a view of her backyard through the matching oval windows above her desk.

Missy sat on her bed with her math book opened on her lap. She had her headphones on tuned to Sean Mendes for inspiration. Across the room, she had four old pairs of jeans cut up into a zillion pieces. All the back pockets had been carefully removed. The legless seats were carefully folded, while the remaining denim fabric from the legs stretched out in long strips hanging from her desk, her dresser, and her reading chair in the corner of her room.

© Melissa A. Borza and CA 2017

M. A. Borza, *Fashion Figures*, DOI 10.1007/978-1-4842-2274-4_5

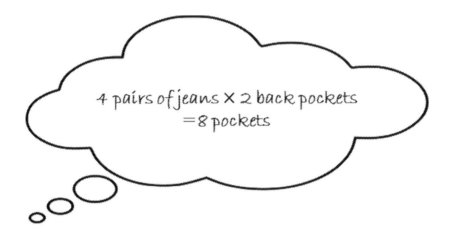

*Four pair times two pockets mean eight pockets to adorn the skirt.* She might be able to make that work. Missy imagined the circumference of the skirt she was designing and using her mental math skills calculated that she was one pocket short. Her original calculations had suggested she would need nine pockets, but should she change the design or find another pair of old jeans at the thrift store or in her dad's closet? Missy wondered.

Missy sketched alternate versions of her design in the margins of her math notebook. "I bet I can make it work, even with seam allowances," Missy said out loud as she worked.

Seam allowances are extra fabric needed for sewing multiple pieces of fabric together. If she didn't add the seam allowances, then her outfit would be smaller than she wanted it to be. Missy had learned that lesson the hard way during her first summer at Camp Winnebago's Maker Camp. She made a pair of spandex shorts that only fit her because the fabric was so stretchy. Her sewing instructor explained the problem. In order to sew a pattern to size, it had to be cut slightly larger than the size it was made for. Missy's problem was that she had cut her pattern to her exact size without adding the seam allowances. So, on her next try Missy cut out a second pair of shorts with an extra quarter inch all around, and those shorts ended up fitting her perfectly—and comfortably.

Missy daydreamed of dancing denim skirts prancing down the imaginary runway in her mind moving in time to the music on her headphones. Bringing her back to math, Pi leapt onto Missy's bed and snuggled his way under Missy's math notebook looking to wriggle his way into Missy's lap. Pi settled there for a moment while Missy stroked his soft, patterned fur, only to be disturbed by the sudden vibrations of Missy's smartphone. Startled, Pi and Missy both jumped, sending pencils, books, sketches, homework, and denim remnants flying in every direction.

"Epic math test tomorrow," Missy read the first part of AJ's group text out loud.

**Brain on fire from studying. :S.**

Missy laughed and held her phone an arm's length away trying to take a selfie that included the mess of papers on her bed and floor—keeping herself and Pi in the center. She replied with a photo and comment.

**Totally. ;) Can't wait 'til it's over! So psyched for Figures and Icons meeting.**

**I think I've got some super ideas!**

In response, the selfie storm started.

Morgan sent a photo of herself sitting at her desk peeking over a stack of books.

**#CHAPSciFi, too! :O.**

CHAPSciFi was the hashtag for the middle school's science and literature fair, and all project proposals were due on Friday. Morgan, AJ and Missy had teamed up last year for the fifth grade science fair. They came in first place for their project, which demonstrated that many brands of so-called flushable wipes were, in fact, not flushable or environmentally friendly at all. In middle school, teams were not allowed, so everyone had to submit proposals for unique science projects or outlines for science fiction stories that imagined how the world might be in a future time.

The selfies continued to arrive on Missy's phone—each with a distinctive *ding, ring, dong* or song. Mahdavi shared a close-up of her hands, fingernails bitten to nubs. Missy took one look and turned her phone away. "Ouch," she said to Pi, "that looks painful."

Danny jumped in and sent a photo of his wide-opened eye with a raised eyebrow. He admonished them.

### Ya'll better keep your eye on the ball.

Missy laughed out loud as she leaned over the side of her bed to grab up the fallen papers and books. She was hanging half on and half off her bed when Mr. Maker knocked and then walked into her bedroom.

"Whoa," he said. "Looks like a tornado came through here!"

"Not quite," said Missy pushing herself up one-handed, while clutching papers with the other hand. "It was Pi!"

Mr. Maker bent down and picked up a handful of note pages. "Interesting designs, Miss. How's math adding up?"

Avoiding his gaze, Missy said, "To sum up, I'm dividing my time between math homework and designing so I don't get bored."

"Ah. Good one," Mr. Maker handed the pages back to Missy and surveyed her bedroom.

Missy righted herself on her bed and started organizing her papers and books.

"Maybe you should work at your desk, kiddo," Mr. Maker suggested, "though that might require more division of labor."

"I'm fine, Dad," Missy said. Her desk was covered in denim cut-outs and she didn't want to go to the trouble of moving and reorganizing all the pieces she had expertly extracted. It had taken more than an hour to lay everything out in the current pattern, which alternated the fronts and backs of the denim strips. It made a really cool effect that she knew the other Figures and Icons members would go crazy for.

"OK," he said, resigned. "After dinner, you can relocate to the dining room table to get your homework done. I really think you need a few less distractions."

Missy nodded, agreeing with her father just as another selfie popped up on her smartphone screen. AJ posed pretending to be unconscious, her math book covering her face. The caption she read made Missy raise her eyebrows and look at her dad in appeal while showing him her screen.

**RIP. Here lies AJ Dupre. Died of a serious math overdose.**

"Looks like AJ needs a resuscitation! Two minutes," he said as Missy started to dial AJ's number. "Dinner in thirty," he said leaving the room as he heard AJ answer on her end.

"OMG!" AJ shouted. "I really think my head is going to explode."

"You'll be fine," Missy assured her.

"Hey, were those pockets you were drawing on your math notes? They looked so cute!" AJ commented.

Missy turned the page with her sketch around in her hand, looking at it from an odd angle. "I'm just playing with an idea. I like the geometry of the triangles and creating visual contrast using different patterns," Missy said.

"Well, I can't wait to see the final design! You're such an inspiration."

Missy blushed, thankful she had phoned rather than video chatted. "We'll see," she said. "BTW, this is your wake-up call! You simply cannot DIE of math!"

AJ giggled. "Thanks, Missy! I know I can count on you to get me through!"

"That's what friends are for." Missy lowered her voice in an imitation of a robot, "Besides, my dad says we need to stay on track with math to be sure we keep all our options open for the best careers when we get older."

AJ laughed and reminded Missy, "If it wasn't for your help, I never would have made it into the advanced math class, anyway."

"It's your hard work keeping you there," Missy said. "Now back to it!" Missy ended the call and considered her own options. She could study more or work on her design in the few minutes before dinner. She gathered up her books and stuffed them in her backpack—she'd had enough math for now. She wanted to play around with her design to see how to avoid looking for another denim pocket. Missy pulled out her tape measure, made some measurements and jotted them down. Then she started on a calculation using the length of the straight tops on the pockets. When she realized what she was doing, she threw her pencil down. *I'm not using math to do this*, Missy decided. *Who needs math for fashion?*

Just as she was settling in at her desk, Missy heard the *dong* that signaled a video call coming from Molly. She had forgotten about their weekly call. Missy uncovered the mouse to click the Accept Call button as she greeted her sister. "Molly, I almost forgot it was Sunday!" she said.

"Hey, Miss. What's up? And why is my screen blocked? Is your webcam on?" Molly asked.

"OMG!" Missy said, exasperated. "I've got a project laid out and," she explained as she carefully picked up the denim strips to reveal her webcam, "I guess it's blocking your view."

"Nice," Molly said. "Looks like you've been busy." As Missy straightened and repositioned the webcam, Molly got a quick preview of the fabric laid out on Missy's desk along with a close-up view of Missy's left hand. "Okay. That's better," Molly commented once Missy had secured the webcam at the top of her monitor.

"I'm working on a design idea for Figures and Icons," Missy reported. "I am thinking about geometric shapes and creating patterns with contrasting the right side with the wrong side of the fabrics. And, I'm still kind of stuck on the idea of using recycled materials and notions. I really like that I can be 'green' and still create something brand new. I even have an idea for some accessories!" Missy reached under her desk and pulled up one of the legless, pocket-less pairs of jeans and wiggled them in front of the camera. Molly's eyes opened wide as she tried to take in exactly what Missy was showing her. "Hey, not so close! I can't see—OK—now I get it. So cool. I mean S-E-W cool!"

"Oh. Now you're channeling Dad, too," Missy smiled at her sister and continued with her explanation. "I'm going to sew the legs closed and add some embellishments with the glue gun and a long strap to transform this into a messenger bag. What do you think?" Missy asked Molly.

Molly squinted and pulled her head back, trying to get a better view. "Wow, Miss! I'm really impressed. I may even place an order for one of your custom bags for myself. Have you told Dad about your concepts? I bet he's thrilled to hear you've been listening all these years about being green!" Missy loved her video chats with Molly, but wished she could spend more time with her in person. As Molly talked, Missy examined her sister's face. She still looked the same—same blond hair as Missy's, though Molly's hair was straight and she kept her long hair down which showed off her amazing green eyes. Missy worried when everyone had said that college would change her, so Missy was always relieved to see that Molly still looked the same.

"It isn't easy being green," Missy mimicked her dad and they both laughed. "Right now, Dad's worried that I'm not focusing enough on my school work."

Onscreen, Molly looked away and yelled over her shoulder, "Yes! I'll be down in a sec." Then she turned back and said to Missy, "School is really important too and you're so smart! I know you can balance your passions and your commitments. I love your ideas and Dad will, too. Anyway, I've gotta run. We are off to the dining hall for dinner. Love ya!"

"Love ya, too," Missy answered, and her screen went black.

After hanging up, Missy's heart ached for just a second. She really missed her big sister, even though she treasured their weekly video chats. Still, she counted the days until Molly would be home for her next break. Missy wished Molly could see her designs up close, feel the weight of the fabric and even try one of them on. She would make her a hobo bag and send it to her.

Missy thought about what Molly had said. She never felt smart, though school-work did seem to come easy to her. Lately, though, everything felt like a distraction pulling her away from what she had discovered she truly loved—creating new designs!

"Dinnnnner!" Missy's dad sang from the kitchen.

"Coming, Dad," Missy responded as she finished pinning her pockets together, without bothering to measure or to make any calculations as she went.

## FASHION HACK: SEAM ALLOWANCE

How do you calculate a seam allowance? The small space of fabric between the raw edge of the material and where the seam is actually sewn is the seam allowance. Common seam allowances range from one-quarter of an inch to as much as several inches. Woven fabrics can easily fray, so the seams on those fabrics need to be sewn far enough away from the raw edge for security and to avoid having gaping holes in your garment.

To be sure your garment will fit to size, add at least one-half inch to all of your measurements before cutting out your pattern pieces. That one-half inch adds one-quarter inch to each end of your fabric, which helps ensure that you can wear your garment after it has been sewn together.

**Good advice: Cut just once AFTER you've measured TWICE.**

# Garbage In ≠ Garbage Out

"EEEP. EEEP. EEEP. EEEP. EEEP." Missy came awake through a fog of exhaustion as she slammed her fist on the button of her radio alarm clock. She sat up and looked around her room. Missy sighed heavily.

For three straight nights, she had stayed up late sewing and ripping apart the same skirt. The denim strips that had been neatly laid out before were now strewn all over her bedroom. The rest of the skirt fabric lay in a heap on the floor under her sewing machine. Missy had thrown it there in a fit of anger the night before.

"Up and at 'em," Missy mumbled to herself. She was channeling G-ma in order to motivate herself to get out of bed. As soon as she set her feet on the floor, she heard her father call goodbye to her from the stairwell. She said goodbye and sleepwalked through breakfast, getting dressed and riding the bus to school. She wondered how she would make it through the day. Missy had never felt this tired in her life.

The first bell rang just as Missy stepped past Mrs. Towers to enter her homeroom class. Missy had health this semester, which was taught by the gym teachers. After her restless night, Missy was tired and mismatched. She had left her house without posting her #OOTD and had noticed on the bus ride that even her pigtails seemed to be drooping. Missy tugged one pigtail north as she dragged herself to her seat and noticed a note on the whiteboard in the front of the classroom: **R U Ready? Recycling Assembly Today**.

© Melissa A. Borza and CA 2017
M. A. Borza, *Fashion Figures*, DOI 10.1007/978-1-4842-2274-4_6

Missy laughed to herself to see the missing letters from the last recycling promotion poster repeated on the board.

Other students caught sight of the note. Soon the whole class was chattering away. Missy yawned widely. She wondered which classes would be suspended while the assembly was held.

Mrs. Towers closed the door and picked up the remote for the class TV. "OK. Settle down," Mrs. Towers said. "Let's hear today's announcements and then we will head to the school assembly."

As the class settled down to listen, Missy noticed that Mrs. Towers wore her usual uniform of CHAPS-wear. She had on a gray sweatshirt and matching sweatpants both emblazoned with the school logo. Topping it all off was a silver whistle dangling from a black cord hung around her neck. Mrs. Towers clicked the remote and the CHAPS-TV channel came on. Three girls from the third grade led the school in the "Pledge of Allegiance," then Chris Jones came onscreen to talk about the all-school assembly, which would be held in the school's auditorium from 8:30 to 10:00 that morning. First-period classes were suspended and all other classes would be shortened by ten minutes, except lunch.

When the video concluded, Mrs. Towers announced, "This will be a great assembly! Pay attention, because students will be expected to develop new ideas for the Reduce, Reuse, Recycle and Repurpose program. So, be inspired and enjoy the assembly!"

Missy half-expected Mrs. Towers to blow her whistle when she finished speaking. Instead, Mrs. Towers used arm motions to direct the students to line up and then walk over to the common campus building, where the school auditorium was located.

For school assemblies, each grade sat together; so, Missy and AJ found their way to each other and pulled in the Figures and Icons friends they saw to sit with them.

The assembly turned out to be a performance by the Green Team Theatre Troupe, or GT3. They performed a tale of two schools—one that didn't recycle and one that did. Both schools started out the same. Over the years, the non-green school spent so much money on waste disposal and replacement purchases that it could no longer afford the latest technologies, new books and important materials for its students, and the upkeep of its buildings. Meanwhile, the school that focused on reducing waste, reusing and repurposing older materials and recycling in other ways had plenty of money for new technologies and top-notch labs and facilities. The green school also encouraged its students to develop innovative programs to continually improve their green-status. Over time, the green school and its students were able to help the failing non-green school to recover by showing them how to be greener.

Missy couldn't help but laugh out loud, when the troupe's narrator closed the show by saying, "It isn't easy being green, unless you and you and you (he pointed to individuals all throughout the audience) and you and you and me JUMP IN!" At those final words, the whole troupe jumped to center stage and dance music blared over the speakers. "Jump! Jump! Jump in!" they chanted in tune with music. The students cheered and the show ended with the curtains closing and all the students dancing in the aisles.

"I'm so pumped!" Morgan said as they headed back to their classes. "I never thought I could be so excited by recycling," she added.

"I know it. Me too," AJ said.

The show had invigorated Missy, though she had been quiet. "I wonder," she started, feeling a new energy pumping her up.

"What's that, Miss?" Danny asked.

"What if we made Figures and Icons all about recycling for this whole year?" Missy pondered. "I mean, we did a great job on our first fashion competition. And, we didn't even HAVE to use old and recycled materials. What if we make using old clothes or donated fabric like part of our charter or something?"

Danny scratched his head, "I like it! It could work. We should talk to Mrs. Frisch to see what she says."

"I'm thinking we could do even more," Morgan said. "What if we start a mending club? That could help too. We could be greener and be helpful to others and maybe get some fabric donations that way too."

AJ and Missy nodded. "Cool!" they exclaimed together. "JINX!" they both said. Then AJ and Missy spent a minute on the Jinx game. Jinx was a longtime favorite game played by Missy and her friends. It could only be played when two people said the exact same word at the exact same time. Whenever that happened, whoever declared "Jinx!" first won the game and silenced the other person.

In order to be released from the jinx, another person had to call the jinxed person by name. In this round, Missy and AJ had not only said matching words but also declared matching jinxes, which extended the game into a kind of overtime. "I love that too," Missy finally said, after winning the jinx and silencing AJ until someone said her name.

Danny took pity on AJ who was rocking back and forth on her heels and seemed ready to jump out of her skin from excitement. He said, "AJ? What's that?"

AJ high-fived Danny and said, "Let's talk to Mrs. Frisch after school and see what she says!" They all agreed, then split up to get to their second-period classes.

Missy shuffled her way through her morning classes eager to get to lunch to talk to her friends about their upcycling ideas. As she walked into her math class, she remembered the scheduled test. Her heart skipped a beat and she held her breath for a moment then blew it out. It was too late to study and too silly to panic. Missy would have to make do with what she knew AND what she did not know. She looked down at her feet and walked to her seat. On the plus side, the test would have to be short since all her classes were abbreviated because of the assembly.

When the lunch bell rang, Missy looked down at her math test and noticed she still had three problems to complete. Where had the time gone? She quickly read the remaining questions and jotted down her answers without taking the time to show her calculations, as the instructions had directed her to do.

Ms. Jameson cleared her throat to get the attention of the last few students still working. "Wrap up, boys and girls. Class has ended."

The remaining students handed their tests to Ms. Jameson, packed up their belongings and filed out of the room. Missy was the last one to hand in her test.

"Everything OK?" Ms. Jameson asked Missy. Missy usually finished her assignments and tests much more quickly, often ahead of everyone else in the class.

"Oh. Yes," Missy answered looking dazed and still wondering how the time had gotten away from her.

"OK. Off to lunch then," Ms. Jameson said.

Members of the fashion club congregated in the hallway outside the art studio, and Morgan and Missy filled them in on their idea to make incorporating recycled and repurposed fabrics into their designs as a theme for the year.

Paula had a few reservations. "I'm not sure that will work for the whole year," Paula explained. "Last year, we had a challenge that required alternative materials—like not even fabric. Some teams used hardware and others used office supplies—it was super awesome and crazy. I remember that the winning look was made entirely out of rope and pieces of colorful garden hoses!"

Missy's jaw dropped. She was speechless. The belt that Ivy made for the first challenge came to mind and other images started dancing in her head. The idea of alternative fabrics really excited her. AJ poked her in the ribs to get her attention. "Whaaa?" Missy asked, coming back to the conversation. "Oh. Sorry," she added closing her mouth and listening.

Kate chimed in, "Really? That sounds super cool. I wonder if those kinds of materials could be collected from recyclables too."

Missy turned away from the group when she heard the click-click of Mrs. Frisch's taupe pumps coming down the hallway. Mrs. Frisch sported a fuchsia sheath dress with a subtle pattern of polka dots that could only be seen when the light reflected off the material. An artful scarf with silver threads running through it draped her shoulders and accented her perfectly made-up face. She wore her hair in a stylish bun with two chopsticks crisscrossed at the base. As usual, Mrs. Frisch was looking totally fab.

"Hello Figures and Icons," Mrs. Frisch sang as she unlocked the classroom. "Welcome! I'd like to hear your ideas about fundraising and planning for our next competitions."

The students poured into the room, excitedly speaking over each other.

Paula stepped to the front of the room and cleared her throat. "Ok. We've got a few big things to talk about today," she started, "but before we jump into that, I know we all want to hear the comments from the judges on our True To You designs."

On cue, Mrs. Frisch handed out the scorecards to the teams who had already paired up around the room. "As you review the judges' remarks and comments, remember that feedback is a gift," Mrs. Frisch told the students. "The judges loved all the designs and want to help us improve as we progress through other challenges this year."

The teams reviewed the scorecards silently, handing them back and forth between team members.

"Please let me know if you have any questions or if there is anything that you don't understand," Mrs. Frisch said.

AJ and Missy scanned their scorecard and read the comments.

"Great, fresh look!"

"Modern and fun."

"Excellent sewing."

"Love the inspired reuse of fabrics!"

"OK. Moving on," Paula announced as the chatter picked up around the room. "Fundraising."

Morgan raised her hand. When Paula called on her, she explained the mending club idea. The students discussed how they could raise money and help other students not only to be more green but also to continue to wear their favorite pieces of clothing even though a repair was needed. After some debate, the students agreed that they could charge a small fee—one dollar for sewing on buttons and two dollars for sewing on patches and doing other minor repairs. The plan was to take in items to be repaired after school one day a week. Depending on how much work they received, the club would get together after school, do the sewing and patching, and return the items one week later. They hoped they could raise one hundred dollars over the course of the year that they could use for notions, small accessories and maybe an end-of-year party.

"I'll make an online form so we can keep track of the mending club activities, like the work we get, who does the sewing and how much money we make," said Morgan.

"I love that idea," Mrs. Frisch commented. "Let's make it official and vote on it!"

The club unanimously accepted the mending club fundraising idea, and Kate, Mahdavi and Danny agreed to get permission to use a corner of the library as a receiving point and to set up the logistics, while AJ committed to promoting it around the school and online.

"Next, we want to run something by you, Mrs. Frisch," Paula said "We were all so inspired by GT3 at today's assembly. We think we can make a positive impact by using recycled materials for all of our challenges this year. What do you think?"

"Wow! What a great concept!" Mrs. Frisch said.

"Do you think we can use recycled materials for the alternative materials competition?" Paula asked.

"I do!" Mrs. Frisch responded excitedly. "That challenge will be next month, and the theme is Green-Piece. Teams will have to use items like recycled plastic, cans, cardboard and paper to create designs. So, I think your concept can work for this and all the other challenges, too" Mrs. Frisch explained.

Danny raised his hand and Paula called on him. "Are you serious? We have to use garbage?" he asked with a look of disgust. "Really?" Danny had been onboard with the idea of reusing donated fabrics and repurposing old clothing, but the thought of using garbage had changed his mind.

"Well, yes," Mrs. Frisch answered. "But the point of the alternative materials challenge is that you will need to transform the so-called garbage into a wearable, lovely garment! What better way to recycle something than to create something beautiful?"

"Hmmm," Danny pondered the idea, not completely sold on it. He crossed his arms in front of his chest. "In any case, we'll need to set up the mending station for accepting clothes needing repairs. I can work on that," Danny commented. "I'll have to do some more thinking on this whole garbage thang," he stage-whispered to Mahdavi with an extra twang of his accent.

"Maybe we can put out a box to take donations near the mending area?" he asked out loud.

"Oooh! Not too near," Mahdavi commented, "that could be disastrous!"

"Gosh! You're right!" Missy laughed at the thought of well-loved items coming in for repair but ending up remade into something completely new.

"OK," said AJ. "I can put a call out on our SocialMe pages and add an announce-ment on CHAPS-TV. I'm on it," she concluded, making a note in her notebook.

The club discussed the challenges set for each of the competitions ahead. Then they shared and discussed designs, sketches and ideas until the meeting concluded.

Missy noticed her friends Megan and Kim passing by the art room. She wondered where they were heading to in such a hurry. AJ poked Missy in the ribs, pointing at the opened door, and whispered, "Where are those two off to in such a rush?"

"No idea," Missy said, though her curiosity was piqued.

When the meeting ended, Missy and AJ meandered down the hallway. When they neared Ms. Jameson's classroom, they slowed down to listen at the open door. Peter Ng, the math club president, was speed-reading math problems and calling out student names for the answers.

*Twenty-three point seven, Missy calculated.* Then she heard a mathlete respond, "Twenty-three point seven."

"Right," said Peter who quickly went on to read the next problem and to call on another mathlete.

*Six hours and twelve minutes.*

"Six hours and twelve minutes," came another response.

Missy answered a dozen questions correctly in her head before AJ tugged her elbow and whispered, "Why don't you join them? I know you'll love it!" AJ said.

"Nah," said Missy walking toward the end of the hall. "It's not for me."

## FASHION HACK: HOBO BAG HOW-TO

1. Find an old pair of jeans and an adult-sized belt that you want to remake (get permission from your parents!).

2. Cut off the legs at a slight angle, being careful to NOT cut the pockets on the back or the pocket liners of the front pockets.

3. Sew or staple the leg openings closed. To hide the seams, you can sew or staple from the inside of your bag by turning the piece inside-out.

4. Thread the belt through only the front and side loops (not the back), fasten the buckle and voila! You have a long strap to carry your bag. You could also use an old necktie or a thin scarf and knot it closed.

5. Add buttons or ribbons or use fabric paint to create a design on it. Have fun while you embellish your bag to make it your own!

# Teasing Out the Answers

All month long, students heard reminders to support the mathletes at their upcoming meet. Even though CHAPS was known for its high-caliber academics, all non-sport activities had to beg for supporters besides parents to show up to events. As the math event got closer and closer, the halls buzzed with chatter about the upcoming basketball game against their rivals from St. Mark's Academy.

M. A. Borza, *Fashion Figures*, DOI 10.1007/978-1-4842-2274-4_7

On Tuesday, Missy noticed another yellow note stuck on her locker. "Need advice. K + M," Missy read. Missy scratched her head, at first thinking "K + M" might be a code to crack; then she realized that it was a message from Kim and Megan. She exchanged some books from her backpack and locker and headed around the corner to look for them. Missy passed by Paula who directed her to Ms. Jameson's math classroom. When Missy got to them, Kim and Megan were sitting cross-legged by the door reviewing a long page of math problems. Missy had gone through elementary school with the two girls and had stayed friends with them even though they had different interests.

"Hey," she said by way of greeting, and the two girls looked up.

"Oh! Missy! Please, please join the math club!" Megan said and pulled Missy down by her hand into a crouched position. "We really need more girls, and we could use your elite skills."

Missy blushed and nearly toppled over. "Whoa," she said and righted herself into a more stable position. "Your note said that you needed advice. How can I help? And don't say by joining the math club!"

"Well," Kim said, exchanging looks with Megan, "we think someone is acting like a bully on the math team. We don't want to get anyone in trouble, but we don't want to be bullied or watch others be bullied either."

"OMG!" Missy said. "That's awful! Why do you think I can help?"

Kim looked down at her hands and fidgeted with her pencil. "I just remember that you used to be bullied . . . I mean, I don't want to make you feel bad, but I thought maybe you could tell us how you managed it and maybe what to do."

Missy let go of Megan's hand and leaned in closer to the girls. She suddenly felt dizzy and on the verge of tears. "I guess you're right. I used to be called 'Missy-Math-Maker.' It started with one boy calling me that and then others picked it up and repeated it and repeated it. And, then it kind of stuck." Missy paused, thinking back to just last year and elementary school. Missy wrapped her arms together holding her stomach, which suddenly felt tight, as she remembered how upset she had been by all the teasing.

"It was really hard for me. It made me feel bad about myself just for being a good student. I know that's weird, but . . .," Missy's voice trailed off, she did not want to admit that she still struggled with those memories and feelings.

"We remember," Megan said. "I felt terrible for you."

"Is someone calling you names?" Missy asked, turning the topic around so she didn't feel so exposed. "You have to tell a teacher or a guidance counselor or the principal!" Missy exclaimed.

"I know it. Right?" Megan said. "That's what I said we should do, too," she looked at Kim who nodded in agreement. "It's just that we don't want to get anyone on the team in trouble."

"If you're talking about the math team, then you should start by talking to Ms. Jameson. I know she will listen and help you," Missy advised. "You know CHAPS has a zero tolerance policy against bullying, right? If you tell her, I know she can solve the problem."

The first bell rang and the girls gathered their books and papers and stood up. "Thanks, Missy!" Megan said. "I do feel better."

"Yes," Kim added. "I knew you could help us!"

The three girls exchanged quick hugs and then dashed to their first-period classes. Missy was glad she could help, though she felt sad remembering all the teasing that she had lived through.

## FASHION HACK: T-SHIRT GROCERY SACK HOW-TO

1. Find an old adult-sized extra-large t-shirt with a great graphic on it.

2. Cut handles by cutting off the arms. Then cut a deep U-shape around the front and back of the neckline.

3. Cut fringe along the bottom of the t-shirt and tie the fringe into knots along the edge.

# Solutions by Design

By Wednesday, Ms. Jameson had graded their latest math assessment. She shared that three students had "aced" the test. Missy smiled to herself, assuming she must be one of the top three. So, when Ms. Jameson handed her test back, Missy couldn't believe the last page was covered in red ink. Since the instructions had directed the students to show their work, Missy had only received half-credit for the correct answers to the last three questions. Instead of a perfect score, Missy was looking at a bright red C circled in the upper right corner of her test. Tears stung her eyes as she held them back and calculated her numeric grade: *Eight math questions in total. The first five were worth eight points each, and the last three were worth twenty points each, which gave her a score of 70 out of a possible 100.*

© Melissa A. Borza and CA 2017

M. A. Borza, *Fashion Figures*, DOI 10.1007/978-1-4842-2274-4_8

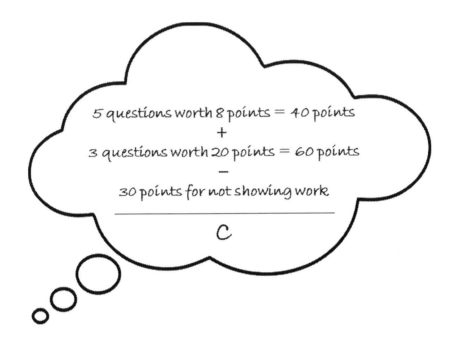

Missy could feel the heat rising from her stomach to her cheeks. She read the note from Ms. Jameson at the top of the first page telling Missy to come see her after school.

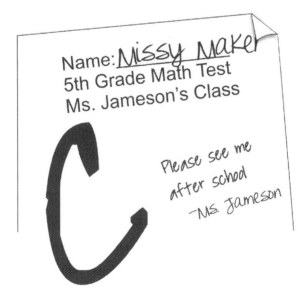

Missy tried to clear her mind by taking a deep breath. She was torn. On the one hand, she didn't want to be known as the geeky girl who always did well in math. She still really wanted to get away completely from the "Missy-Math-Maker" nickname from elementary school; someday, she hoped to be known as Missy Maker—Fashionista. Maybe doing poorly on a math test was not so terrible after all. Maybe this was the year she would ditch that mean "Missy-Math-Maker" moniker once and for all. So, why did she feel like such a failure?

At lunch, most students were talking about the upcoming basketball game including Missy's friends. Missy wondered why so many hours were wasted reviewing the skills of star players and guessing how they would match up against the team from St. Mark's. On the other hand, the only people talking fashion were a few of the Figures and Icons club members; similarly, Missy only heard one passing remark about the Math Olympics where Peter was projecting a shut-out for the CHAPS team.

Missy looked for AJ in the crowded cafeteria. When she couldn't find her, Missy sat with Danny and Mahdavi who cheered her up with their playful banter. Missy loved listening to the two of them talk about anything. Their unique accents were captivating. The two discussed their roles in the CHAPS Marching Band. They reviewed the marching band's playlist and the timing as they would be playing both before the big game and ahead of the math meet to get everyone stoked up. Danny played the trumpet and Mahdavi performed with the color guard. They discussed the band's marching routines and concluded that the whole event would be great fun, if not a little crazy because of the double-booking. The Math Olympics competition was scheduled to follow the basketball game. The two events were being held back-to-back on the CHAPS campus. Mahdavi passed Missy a sketch she and Danny had worked on that included a new idea for their school logo and a redesign of the marching band uniforms.

"Wow. These are so great," Missy commented.

Toward the end of lunch, AJ slid in and squeezed next to Missy on the cafeteria bench. Her eyes were red and puffy. It looked as if she had been crying, though she kept her head down and focused on unwrapping her lunch.

"You OK?" Missy asked in a hushed voice so no one would overhear. Danny and Mahdavi continued chatting away and didn't seem to notice that AJ had joined their table.

"Yeh. I'm fine," AJ answered finally releasing a granola bar from its packaging, hoping to eat it before the bell rang.

"You don't look fine," Missy pressed.

"I don't want to talk about it now," AJ said stuffing a bite of granola into her mouth just as the bell rang.

All afternoon, Missy dreaded her meeting with Ms. Jameson. How could she explain what happened? How would a teacher ever understand the strange problem Missy had? How weird was it that she loved math but didn't want anyone to know about it? Her classes went by in a daze, and at 3 PM, she gathered her books and stopped by her locker to pack up for the night, then headed to Ms. Jameson's room.

Missy was surprised to see Megan and Kim coming out just as she was entering. They exchanged quick greetings and Megan gave Missy a thumbs-up as she pulled the door closed on her way out. Missy guessed they had talked to Ms. Jameson about the bullying situation. Missy was glad she had helped them in some small way.

"Hi, Missy." Ms. Jameson said and directed her to join her at the round table next to her desk. Missy shuffled over and sat down heavily, dropping her backpack to the floor.

"Hi," Missy replied and looked down at the table in front of her.

"So," Ms. Jameson started, "it looks like you had some trouble on the test this week."

"Uh," Missy could not find any words. She fidgeted with her hands for something to do.

"It's clear that you're a very smart girl. I know you can do these math problems. After all, you did get all the answers correct. You just did not follow the clearly stated directions." Ms. Jameson paused to give Missy time to comment. When Missy remained silent, she continued, "I could not give you full credit when you didn't show how you worked through those complex problems. It's great that you arrived at the correct answers, but I have no way of knowing HOW you got there. Do you understand?"

"Yes," Missy said without looking up. She could feel heat rising from her stomach and tears filling her eyes again. She thought she might cry if she said any more. So, she kept her eyes focused on her two hands now resting on the table.

"Now, it's just one test. It's not going to ruin your whole year. Still, I really need to see your work. You need to show how you are addressing the problem and what math concepts you are applying. OK? I need to see that you are not just guessing."

"OK," Missy said still staring at her hands.

"Please look at me," Ms. Jameson said.

That was all it took, as Missy turned her gaze from her hands to Ms. Jameson, the tears started flowing. "OK. I get it. I do. I just lost track of the time. I did all the math in my head and just wrote down my results. I knew I should show my work, but the bell already rang and you were calling for us to turn in the exams."

Ms. Jameson seemed prepared for the tears and handed Missy a tissue box. "Wow. You answered all three questions in a matter of minutes. That's amazing, Missy! You really are a gifted young lady."

Missy dabbed her eyes with the tissue then blew her nose. Right now she didn't feel very gifted, and she was out of words.

"Alright then, I know you will manage your time better and follow the directions more closely in the future. For your homework, please take the time to work through those problems again, this time showing your work and your calculations," Ms. Jameson concluded and handed Missy another tissue. "You might also consider joining the math club, kiddo. You have some special skills."

Missy shook her head at the comment. She composed herself and grabbed her backpack. She threw out her tissues in the garbage pail by Ms. Jameson's desk, then she walked to the exit. Missy took a deep breath and opened the door to find AJ standing at the ready about to knock. They exchanged looks of surprise as Missy exited and AJ entered the classroom.

"Come in, AJ," Ms. Jameson called.

Missy thought about waiting by the door, but didn't want AJ to think she was spying on her. Missy thought she would check out what the mathletes were up to and then try to catch up to AJ before getting her bus home.

Slipping into the mezzanine of the dark auditorium was easier than Missy expected. The only lights lit up a small area on the stage where a table and five chairs stood. Eleven students spread out in the front center two rows. Missy recognized a few friends including Megan and Kim.

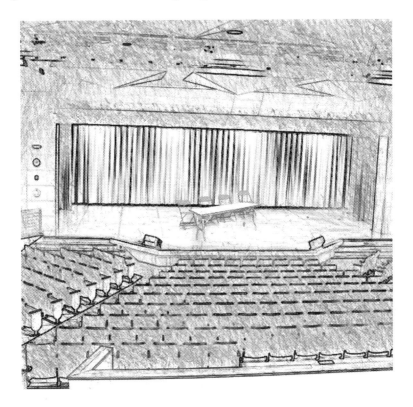

*Fifty feet back from the stage and one story high, Missy wondered why she couldn't hear better as she calculated the speed of sound and the distance it would have to travel to arrive at her ears.* Peter paced in front of the table on the stage. He was saying something, but from her elevation, Missy could only catch an occasional word. "Win ... Olympics ... CHAPS ..." Missy heard Peter saying.

The math team had been meeting and practicing for weeks. CHAPS was hosting the Math Olympics the next weekend. Missy had stayed away until now, but the excitement of the upcoming competition had her friends buzzing though not many people really knew what it was all about. Missy's curiosity had finally won out. She wanted to find out more. She took a seat in the second row of the mezzanine and leaned forward to see if she could hear any better. Suddenly she heard the clickety-click-squeak of a nearby door opening up. She slouched down in her seat so she wouldn't be seen.

Christopher Jones stepped to the front of the mezzanine and waved his hands toward the people on the stage below. He shouted, "Are you talking? Totally cannot hear you up here!"

Chris was practically an icon at CHAPS. He was an eighth grader who had found his calling early with the Audio-Visual Club and managed to first convince the AV department and then the CHAPS school board to upgrade to a modern digital system. He led the efforts to fundraise for it, and he had created a CHAPS-TV channel where the AV Club members anchored school news and shared school announcements every day during homeroom. And, on top of that, Missy thought he was the cutest boy in the school!

Chris had brown eyes. Missy noticed on CHAPS-TV how they sparkled with golden highlights. His light brown hair was long and usually swept back from his face when he was on camera, but off camera it flopped across his forehead and partially hid his eyes. Missy got the sense that Chris wanted to be hiding behind his long hair. He looked to be about five and one-half feet tall, which made him about six and one-half inches taller than Missy. *The perfect boy-to-girl height ratio,* she imagined. Under other circumstances, Missy might have introduced herself or at least said "Hey," but as it was, she was holding her breath, trying to disappear completely and melt into the auditorium floor.

Suddenly, a high-pitched screech pierced the room, interrupting Missy's thoughts. She nearly jumped out of her crouched position. Missy covered her mouth because she thought she had gasped.

"OK!" Chris yelled. "Now, Peter, turn on your mic!"

Missy saw Peter fiddle with a black box pinned on his belt. Then, "How's that? Test 1-2-3. Test. Test," Peter's voice echoed through the auditorium.

"Great," said Chris turning to give a thumbs-up signal to someone who must have been above and behind Missy. "We'll get the rest of the mics on the table and then you'll be good to go."

Chris left the mezzanine and two minutes later showed up on the stage below. Missy sat up taller in her seat relieved that she had not been discovered. She took a deep breath. Missy turned to look back at who or what Chris was signaling to and noticed a light shining toward the stage from a small square hole at the back of the mezzanine. Then she saw some movement and guessed that a few students must be up there working the AV equipment. She blushed, wondering if she had been seen.

Peter returned to pacing and now Missy heard every word over the speakers. "Like I was saying, we've got a good team and with me as your leader, we'll crush this tournament!"

Missy rolled her eyes. Peter was great at math, but winning would be a team effort. She was rooting for her friends, but Peter's comments just rubbed her the wrong way. She wondered if that's what had bothered Megan and Kim.

"Thanks, Peter," Ms. Jameson appeared below and stepped forward to climb the stairs up to the stage. "Isn't this exciting?" she asked turning toward the other students. Missy considered that Ms. Jameson's meeting with AJ must be over, but she stayed in her seat to hear some more.

"Go CHAPS!" Peter pumped his fist in the air, but the other math club members didn't seem to be as enthusiastic. Missy wondered why.

"Hmmm. I can see you're all a bit nervous," said Ms. Jameson. "No need for that! You are all great mathletes and to prove it, why don't we warm up with some times tables." She pointed to the first row at Kim and said, "Come on up, Kim! Lead us in twelves." Kim came up the stairs nearest her and made her way to the center of the stage. Chris appeared from backstage and handed her a microphone. He switched it on and she started, "Twelve, twenty-four, ..." and the math club members joined in.

When Kim got to one hundred forty-four, Ms. Jameson said, "Great! Team, how are we feeling?" and the club members clapped and cheered. "OK, everyone on your feet!" The team stood up. "Peter lead us in fifteens."

Peter, happy to be back in the spotlight, shouted, "Fifteen, thirty," and the club joined in.

When they got to three hundred, Ms. Jameson said, "Perfect! Now that the mics are set up and the stage is set, let's divide into two teams and have a math scrimmage." She used her arm to divide the mathletes into two teams and they all climbed onstage, taking seats at the two tables. Ms. Jameson stood in the middle with her back to the audience.

Ms. Jameson explained that the judges and the announcer would be in the front row for the actual competition. Mathletes were allowed to have one pencil and one notecard in front of them to use as scratch paper. On the stage, a giant countdown clock would face the competitors. They would be allotted thirty seconds for each problem. In the finals, they would be given a full minute to answer the questions. Twelve teams would compete in rounds, with the winning teams advancing to the next rounds until only three teams remained. The last three teams would compete for first place.

"Let's run through a series of problems," Ms. Jameson said and began quizzing the teams, using her smartphone to time them.

Missy whispered the responses to herself seconds before the mathletes below.

"Excuse me?" a voice called from behind her. When Missy didn't respond, Chris came around and tapped her on the shoulder. She jumped.

"Hi. Sorry," Chris said. "The mezzanine is closed. You can watch the team practice from the main auditorium," he said. "By the way, how'd you get those answers so quick? I heard you answer before I heard anyone on the team respond."

Where had he come from? Missy had been so absorbed by the scrimmage, she had not heard any door opening or any footsteps approaching.

"Uh. Oh. Um," Missy stuttered, trying to find her words, suddenly feeling nauseous. "Oh. OK. Thanks," she finally said, standing up and brushing past him while nearly hitting him with her backpack. She quick-stepped her way up the aisle and out the door. She rounded the corner and ducked into the nearest girls' bathroom, leaving Chris standing in the mezzanine looking after her.

Missy stood by the bathroom sink and looked in the mirror. Her cheeks were bright red—just like the C on her math test. She had splashed some water on her face when she heard a sob coming from one of the stalls.

"Hello?" Missy called out.

"M-m-missy? Is that you?" AJ replied while trying to contain her sobs.

"Oh my goodness! AJ, it's me!" Missy answered. "Come out and tell me what's going on!"

AJ came out of the stall and washed her hands and face at the sink. Missy tore off some paper towels from a nearby dispenser and handed them to her friend.

"Oh, Missy! It's awful. I failed that math test. I don't know how it happened. I just panicked. I thought I knew the material. I studied so hard, but I totally flaked and I didn't even get to the last question," AJ said in a rush. "I didn't want to tell you before because I know it's so easy for you and I'm so embarrassed."

Missy pulled AJ in for a hug and then spilled her guts. She confessed how she had lost track of time and flubbed on the last three questions. Soon the two girls were consoling each other and each began to feel better.

Suddenly AJ's face changed and she started to cry again. "But that's not the worst of it!" AJ cried. "My dad said if I can't keep my grades up, I have to drop all my extracurricular activities—including the fashion club and soccer!" AJ ended on a sob.

Missy's stomach turned. How could she keep her friend from failing? How could she help AJ stay in the fashion club and keep playing soccer?

"We can fix this!" Missy promised. "Remember last year? We met in the morning to study and worked on homework together after school? We can do that again! I can help you with math and you can help me stay focused and not get too distracted on fashion and our designs."

AJ smiled, "You would do that for me?"

"Of course!" Missy exclaimed, "You're my best friend and my design partner—we need each other!"

As the two exited the girls' bathroom, Missy recounted her run-in with Chris Jones. AJ raised her eyes, puckered her lips, and made kissing noises. "Love at first sight!" AJ declared and both the girls giggled.

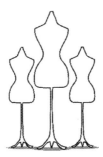

Time was not her friend these days! Missy expected to complete her designs and still get her homework done long before Dad announced "Lights out!" with finality.

This was the third night this week that she had resorted to using her smartphone to light up her textbooks under her covers. How had she gotten behind? Why was she so tired? Missy thought back to what she had been doing these last weeks. Schoolwork, house chores, helping AJ, and . . . Designing! Oh designing was so much fun, and so easy to get lost in.

In her mind's eye, Missy's latest fashions high-stepped down the runway, the last one waving and entreating her forward. Missy followed the dresses, skirts and rompers across the stage and down the runway. She stopped short when she noticed that as the garments reached the end of the runway, rather than pivoting and turning back, they stepped off the edge and exploded into tiny numbers. The numbers rose up before her like a colorful plume of smoke and swirled around her making her feel shaky and dizzy. When the numbers cleared up, she saw Chris standing and applauding in the front row. *One plus one equals perfection.*

Missy awoke to G-ma's gentle shaking. "Wakey, wakey, Miss Melissa Merry Maker. The day's awaiting!"

Disoriented and groggy, Missy awoke and asked, "G-ma, what time is it?"

"Time to get up and start the day, dearie," G-ma said. "Your father called you twice before he left. Now you'll need to hurry if you want to catch the bus."

Missy dressed in a fury, forgetting to check her fashion calendar or her social media feeds until she stopped by her mirror. Despite her brain fog, and racing around, Missy thought she looked pretty good. She had grabbed a pair of striped blue on blue leggings and a long gray t-shirt embellished with tiny round cut-outs on the neckline, hem and shoulders. She had experimented with a grommet-making tool and loved the effect. She added a white belt with a giant metal buckle and cinched it just below her waist. Then she tied her hair up in a quick side braid. Missy snapped a selfie and posted it with the hashtags OOTD and Never2Late4Fashion. She picked up her backpack, and ran down the stairs. G-ma handed her a granola bar as Missy passed through the kitchen and headed out the door to catch the bus to school.

Tired as she was, Missy felt like the day swept past her. Only AJ even noticed the side braid that replaced Missy's usual ponytail or pigtails. They spent lunch drilling math concepts and reviewing their tests to understand where each had made mistakes. AJ was feeling better and had signed up for extra help sessions with Ms. Jameson too. Missy was sure AJ could turn things around and be able to stay involved in her clubs and activities.

Missy had hoped to run into Chris in the hallway between classes just to say hi and to apologize for lurking in the mezzanine, but she never saw him once all day—not even on CHAPS-TV that morning. Meanwhile, all her classmates talked about was the basketball game to be held Saturday. Missy understood the excitement of an impending competition and hoped the whole school would one day be just as excited about the fashion club's meets too!

Missy returned home that evening after an extra-long homework session with AJ. She had missed the late bus and ended up walking the two-point-four miles home. She dropped her pack by the front door and snapped a selfie. Typing hashtag homeatlast and posting that with her picture, Missy climbed the five stairs from the foyer and was met by G-ma, her dad and Ms. Jameson sitting in her family's living room.

Taken aback, Missy exclaimed, "Whoa! It's not my birthday. What's going on?"

Mr. Maker stepped forward. "Missy, we are here for you."

Missy stopped in her tracks. She hadn't yet told her father about her recent math test grade. She suddenly felt betrayed that Ms. Jameson had gone behind her back directly to her father. Even though she was a family friend to Missy's dad, it did not seem fair that Ms. Jameson would blab to Missy's father and then lounge on the sofa in Missy's living room.

Recognizing fear on Missy's face, Ms. Jameson quickly spoke up, "So, I ran into your dad at the supermarket this afternoon, and I mentioned that the mathletes urgently need a stand-in for our math competition on Saturday."

Relieved on some levels, Missy sank into the recliner nearest her and kicked off her trainers nearly hitting Pi with one of them. Pi whipped Missy's legs with his tail in rebuke. Missy scooped up Pi and put the cat between herself and everyone else. She tucked her legs under her bottom and sat in a strange contortion on the leather rocking recliner petting Pi with her cheek as she clutched him to her chest.

"Is something going on?" Mr. Maker asked looking suspiciously from Missy to Ms. Jameson.

"Are you OK, dearie? You look a little pale," G-ma added.

Missy imagined she was being interrogated under a single bare lightbulb. In her mind, she could hear the tick-tock of an old-fashioned clock counting the seconds before her imminent doom. "Um. I don't know," Missy answered. Pi escaped Missy's grasp and jumped down to the floor. "Dad, I-I was going to tell you about my math test. Then, well, with everyone here, I just thought I was in trouble or something."

"You are not in trouble!" Ms. Jameson said. "But the math team is! We need a minimum of twelve people for competition. Since one student dropped out, just today, I need to find someone who can jump right in and be successful on the team. I thought of you and how quickly you can do mental math. It wouldn't be so urgent if CHAPS were not also hosting the event. Without twelve students, we will have to forfeit the competition and still host it. But, if I can find a student to join the team, we can avoid that embarrassment."

Missy resisted asking who had dropped out. Her mind wandered to her conversation with Megan and Kim. Did one of them drop out? Did the bully get called out? She pictured the two rows in the auditorium and tried to guess who from the team was gone.

"So, Missy, what do you think?" Missy's dad asked, pulling her focus back to the discussion. "I know you said you didn't want to join before. And what were you saying about a math test?"

"Oh that was nothing," Ms. Jameson supplied. "Just rushing and not reading directions. Missy and I agreed she would read and follow instructions more carefully from now on."

"Oh. So, Missy, do you think you can help the math team this weekend? It sounds like they really need you," Mr. Maker asked.

G-ma walked over to Missy and patted her shoulder. "You don't have to do this. It is your decision," she said.

Missy rocked back and forth and fidgeted with her hair considering the proposal. "I suppose I can help out this weekend, but I don't want to commit for the whole year. Is that OK?"

Ms. Jameson clapped her hands. "Yes! That will be a huge help to the team. And, who knows, you might like it—and you would be welcome to stay on!"

*One hundred percent chance of staying on the math team minus one hundred percent of interest, meant there was zero percent likelihood of joining the math club on a permanent basis.* Missy promised that she would help out just this once, and Ms. Jameson explained how the competition worked and what to expect over the remaining days leading up to the event.

## MATH HACK: SHORTCUT FOR MULTIPLES OF 11

For this example, let's multiply: 11 x 75 = ?

1.  Add the digits of the number that is being multiplied by 11.

$$7 + 5 = 12$$

2.  Place this sum between the 7 and 5.

$$7 ( 12 ) 5$$

3.  If the sum exceeds 9 like it does in this case, we must carry the one over and add it to the digit on the left. In this case, that means the 7 becomes an 8, the 2 remains in the center, and 5 is the last digit.

$$11 \times 75 = 825$$

# To the Nines

Missy finally made it up to her room. She felt exhausted and overwhelmed. She spread out her homework and books across the comforter on her bed. She read the flyer from Ms. Jameson with details about the math club and Saturday's competition. Then she flicked the blue piece of paper describing the math event like a Frisbee. It flew the length of her bed and then floated down to land upon her pillow near the end of her bed just as Pi entered the room. Pi surveyed the available space on the bed and leapt up. He pranced around, stepping on all the papers and books on Missy's bed, then nudged away the flyer with his nose and settled himself on Missy's pillow. Missy eased herself onto the bed and used her phone to snap candid shots of Pi. Pi cleaned his fur and ignored Missy completely.

Missy slithered back down to floor level trying not to disturb Pi. She knelt on the floor with her elbows leaning on the foot of her bed. Something stirred inside her and she made her decision. She felt excited and worried.

Missy texted AJ, Megan and Kim. **U There?**

**YEP** AJ responded. **Heading out to soccer practice.**

**I'm here :).** Megan texted adding her usual sideways smile, opting to never use the graphical version of the emoji.

Missy sent her three closest friends a picture of Pi with the math club flyer by his front paws to warm up. Then Missy posed with Pi positioned in the background and Missy peeking over her math notebook, which was covered in math formulas and fashion doodles. She snapped the selfie and texted it to all of her friends—mathletes and fashionistas alike. Missy wondered what the other Figures and Icons would say. AJ was her best friend, after all, and always supported her.

© Melissa A. Borza and CA 2017
M. A. Borza, *Fashion Figures*, DOI 10.1007/978-1-4842-2274-4_9

**Guess who's subbing on the math team this weekend!?**

**Wow! That's super.** AJ answered with a series of smiley faces. Catch you after practice.

Kim finally responded with a row of happy emojis and a photo of her own thumbs-up.

**You'll be great!** Danny texted along with a close-up photo of his own face winking into the camera, which spurred a round of other selfies imitating emojis. Danny had a way of cheering Missy up, no matter the situation.

**REALLY?!?** Mahdavi jumped in. **Our design star is a math whiz too? Who knew!**

Satisfied and feeling more at ease about her decision, Missy held her phone out and posed for a selfie with her tongue sticking out and responded to all.

**Super!** Kate answered. Missy laughed, knowing Kate was responding to her original news and certainly not to her last selfie. Kate was too buttoned up for that.

Missy smiled, relieved that her friends did not call her out for being a freak and a math geek. Their responses genuinely seemed to support her participation in the upcoming math competition.

Abruptly overcome with excitement, Missy abandoned her phone and her homework and headed to her closet. Finding the perfect outfit for the Math Olympics suddenly seemed more important than anything else. *Six pants, four skirts and twelve tops means one hundred and twenty possible outfits!*

Missy pulled out her favorite pieces and tossed them on top of the books on her bed causing Pi to hastily take his leave. She arranged three combinations, added accessories and shoes, and snapped pictures of each. She narrowed it down to two pants' outfits and one skirt outfit to choose from.

Missy pictured the auditorium and the table arrangement and quickly tossed the skirt to the floor beside her bed. From the mezzanine, she knew you couldn't see any legs beneath the table, but she wasn't sure about the view from the main auditorium to the stage. She rearranged the tops and accessories and eliminated one top, adding it to the skirt on the floor. She retook her photos and posted them with the hashtags possibleOOTDs and mathfashion.

#possibleOOTDs

G-ma knocked on the open door. "Really cute," she commented on the outfits as she stepped inside Missy's room. G-ma looked at Missy standing in the middle of her bedroom surrounded by books, papers and items of clothing and looking disheveled herself. "Miss Melissa, you feeling OK?" she asked.

G-ma stepped over a heap of papers by the door and sat down on the chair beside Missy's bed. Pi strolled back in and weaved himself through her legs. G-ma petted the cat who promptly pointed his nose in the air and squeezed himself under Missy's bed.

"Well, then!" G-ma said to Pi, patiently waiting for Missy to reply.

Missy looked up from her phone and noticed the mess she had created in her bedroom. "Sorry for the mess," Missy said, scooping up papers and clothes and dropping them on the desk chair behind her.

"I'm ok, G-ma," Missy started. "I want to help Ms. Jameson and the mathletes. I really do. I just . . ."

"What is it?" G-ma prompted her and patted the bed next to her chair. Missy sat down heavily on the bed.

G-ma raised her eyebrows as papers flew up from the bed. "Whoa!" she laughed.

"I don't want to be a geek anymore!" Missy blurted out then jumped up again. She busied herself with picking up the outfits and accessories and hanging them back in her closet.

"Oh! Missy! You are a smart, generous and loving young lady," G-ma said.

Missy stopped in her tracks and shook her head. "ARG! Please don't say that I'm smart," Missy complained. "I don't want to be called smart. I just want to be me." Missy picked up a shirt from the floor and a hanger from her bed and put the two together. She stacked a few hanging garments and lay them over her arms and started across the room.

G-ma stood up and crossed the room. She caught Missy in a hug as Missy walked back empty-handed from her closet toward her bed. "Oh, dearie, being smart *is* being you. You are a great problem-solver *and* a gifted designer. All that is something to be proud of; it's not anything to hide or shy away from."

Missy hugged G-ma back, then pulled away and went back to her work tidying up her room, putting clothes away and avoiding eye contact. She thought if she looked at her grandmother, she might cry. *Eight steps from bed to closet. Two hands, two arms, two shoulders. Four trips to the closet and back. Sixty-four steps.*

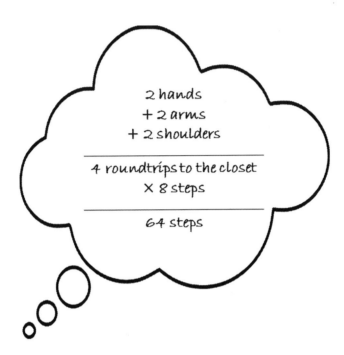

Missy looked at her feet, counting her paces. "You have to say that, G-ma. Besides, you're not in middle school," Missy said, nearly breathless from pacing, bending and picking up articles of clothing.

"You are right about that, dearie. I have not been in school for a long time, but I do know how you feel," G-ma said. "It's hard to be a unicorn. Not everyone appreciates the unique abilities and the special skills you have. They may be jealous or afraid, but that should never ever stop *you* from being the wonderful you that you are." G-ma lifted Missy's chin to look her in the eyes. "You are my unicorn," she said and kissed Missy's cheek.

Missy sat cross-legged on the floor and put her head in her hands. She felt dizzy and confused. She never thought of herself as a unicorn before, but she loved that image. "I *am a unicorn*," Missy repeated to herself.

G-ma put her hand on Missy's shoulder. "You should not hide your best parts to try to make other people like you," G-ma said. "The world needs all your special talents!"

As if on cue, Pi exploded into Missy's lap, sprawling across her legs and batting at Missy's arms with his paws. G-ma leaned over and ruffled Missy's hair. "Your dad ordered pizza for dinner," she said. "Should be here in twenty minutes. OK?" She patted Missy reassuringly and walked to the door. G-ma left Missy's room, and Pi leapt off Missy's lap and followed G-ma out.

Missy stretched out on her bedroom floor and imagined a combined math and fashion competition where each model had to solve math problems at the end of the runway. She pictured Morgan and Kate dressed to the nines followed by Peter and some of the other mathletes, who in Missy's mind's eye were not nearly as fashionable. Each student paraded their way to a microphone at the end of the runway where they were asked to solve a complex math problem. When they answered correctly, the mathletes turned and walked backstage. She giggled at the thought.

Missy opened her eyes, sat up and started reviewing the math worksheets that Ms. Jameson had given her to prepare for the competition. *Dressed to the nines . . .* Missy thought about the expression and laughed. Fashion and math intermingled. No wonder she loved both so well!

## MATH HACK: DIVISION TRICKS

Divide large numbers at top speed!

**3** Divisible by 3 if the sum of the digits of the number are divisible by 3 (492 is because 4 + 9 + 2 equals 15, which is divisible by 3).

**4** Divisible by 4 if the last two digits of the number are divisible by 4 (2676 is because 76 is a multiple of 4).

**6** Divisible by 6 if the rules of divisibility for 2 and 3 work for that number (804).

**9** Divisible by 9 if the sum of digits of the number are divisible by 9 (5922 because 5 + 9 + 2 + 2 equals 18, which is divisible by 9).

**12** Divisible by 12 if the rules of divisibility for 3 and 4 work for that number (1068 is because 1 + 0 + 6 + 8 = 15, which is divisible by 3, and 68 is a multiple of 4).

# All the Right Angles

Friday evaporated in a haze. As Missy donned her final mathfashion OOTD—a mash-up of a blue t-shirt emblazoned with gold-sequined math symbols, the denim skirt she created from jeans' pockets, paired with leggings and her favorite black trainers—she tried to recall where she had spent her time on Friday. Between cramming for the competition and scrimmaging with the math team, all she could remember was the excitement building up and then just waking up today and feeling slightly out of sorts.

"Missy? You ready?" Mr. Maker called from the hallway. "We should get going!"

Missy was ready. She checked her look and re-tied her ponytail in a position lower than usual. Her ponytail hung at the back of her head right below the equator where she imagined the Indian Ocean might be. She thought the low ponytail made her appear more serious and ready for the competition. One quick selfie and she was off. "Coming, Dad!" she shouted as she closed her bedroom door behind her.

© Melissa A. Borza and CA 2017
M. A. Borza, *Fashion Figures*, DOI 10.1007/978-1-4842-2274-4_10

light blue t-shirt
with golden math symbols

+

denim skirt made
with jean pockets

+

light blue leggings

+

favorite black sneakers

=

# Final mathfashion OOTD

Missy hopped into the front seat and buckled her seat belt. Ever since she started middle school, Missy had wanted to ride up front. Mr. Maker winked at her. "Nice try, kiddo. Back seat, please. When you reach five feet tall, we'll negotiate. Until then, the back seat is safest." Mr. Maker smiled and waited for Missy to exit.

"Oh, Dad," Missy whined as she complied. Missy unbuckled and opened the front door. She settled into the back seat, buckled up and looked up into the rearview mirror. "Okay. Ready, Dad."

"We're off!" Mr. Maker declared and started the car.

In the car, Missy posted her selfie to her SocialMe timeline and felt a twang in her heart when she read a post on her page: **CHAPS Mathletes make way—Missy-Math-Maker saves the day!** Missy had worked hard to separate herself from that name. She wanted to be known as a fashionista, not a math geek.

That post was followed by replies from her friends.

**Go Missy!** said Kate.

**You got this, girl,** from Danny.

**Missy, you are a math wizard,** said Mahdavi.

**CHAPS for the win!** from Paula.

Missy was torn. The use of the Missy-Math-Maker nickname she had been bullied with all through elementary school felt like an assault. She had worked so hard this year to escape that moniker. On the other hand, the post was praising her. Wasn't it? Still, her spirits lifted and she felt exalted by her friends. "Hmmm. Missy-Math-Maker: M-cubed," Missy said, embracing the dreaded label and rebranding herself in mathematical terms.

**Ready! Willing! And able!** Missy responded and signed $M^3$ then she turned off her phone and concentrated on the ride through her town. She counted the street signs and imagined mixing them all up. She wondered if returning residents would still be able to find their way home.

It was a quick ride to the CHAPS campus early on a Saturday morning. Normally, the ride to school took more than thirty minutes. On school days, the roads were clogged with traffic and her school bus made eight stops along the way.

"Wow," Missy commented. She looked at her phone to confirm the time. "We got here in twelve minutes!"

Mr. Maker winked at Missy. "No delays today," he replied. Mr. Maker was dressed as usual in a button-down shirt, bow tie and jeans. Missy thought of that as her dad's uniform, though on the weekends, he wore sneakers instead of loafers. That was his casual look.

Missy wondered if her sense of style had anything to do with her dad's unique daily uniform. He always left the house put together and even his most casual outfits included a button-down shirt and a bow tie. Missy gathered up her papers and pencil from her seat taking her time as her dad parked the car. Missy looked in the rearview mirror and waited to catch her dad's eye. Missy felt a fluttering in her stomach and caught her breath. "Dad? I'm a bit nervous."

Mr. Maker turned around in his seat. "Here's a question: Why is six afraid of seven?" he asked.

"Huh?" Missy responded with a confused look on her face. "What? Dad, what are you talking about?"

"Because . . ." Mr. Maker dragged out the word to build suspense before responding, "seven ATE nine! HAH!"

Missy rolled her eyes at her father and smiled in spite of herself.

"You'll be great, kiddo!" Mr. Maker said. "A little nervous energy makes you sharp. Just have fun and remember this: math is awesome and so is Missy Maker!"

Missy repeated that mantra under her breath as she opened the car door and headed toward the auditorium. "Math is awesome and so is Missy Maker. Math is awesome and so is Missy Maker. Math is awesome and so is Missy-MATH-Maker!" Missy chanted to herself.

Mr. Maker and Missy got out of the car together. "I'll meet you after the competition," Mr. Maker said. Missy noticed the school parking lot was filling up with buses and cars filled with students from other schools. Students were looking around trying to figure out where to go to register for the event.

They approached the side door to the building, Danny came running out, calling to Missy. He was wearing a band uniform jacket and gym shorts with flip-flops. Mr. Maker kissed Missy on the cheek.

"Whoa!" Mr. Maker said as Danny approached them.

"Hey, Mr. Maker," Danny said.

"Hey to you, Danny."

Danny stopped and looked Missy over from head to toe. He snapped his fingers in a Z configuration. "You look snaz-zy! And, thank heaven you're here!" Danny said, his southern accent exaggerated to the fullest extent. "I was waiting for you, Missy! We've had a wardrobe malfunction and I know you can help."

"I'll see you after the competition," Mr. Maker told Missy and headed to the main entrance. Danny took Missy's hand and pulled her into the building and down the hall toward the band room.

When they entered the band room, Missy saw articles of clothing and pieces of band uniforms strewn all over. The band director was in a tizzy directing students and tuning instruments. He was so busy reviewing the band choreography and marching drills that he barely noticed the chaos in the room. The director had on a full band uniform including a tall stovepipe hat, which seemed ready to fall from its perch if not for the chin strap holding it in place.

Other band members were in various states of dress, some were playing their instruments, and others were shouting to each other trying to locate a full uniform. They looked so motley and mismatched. Suddenly, Missy's jitters were gone. She loved the chaos and clutter; it magically calmed her nerves.

Mahdavi ran past them and out the door. She wore a white tank top tucked into her black band uniform pants.

Thomas Barker, Missy's neighbor and friend since the first grade, wore a full uniform, with the red and gold jacket hanging open. With only two buttons, there was no way to keep it closed. No two band members seemed to be dressed alike. Clearly, the band was in trouble.

"How can I help?" Missy asked, just as Mahdavi came back into the room pulling Megan and Kim beside her. Megan's hair was braided from the left side above her ear all the way across her forehead and tucked in place in the back of her right ear, wrapping her head like a crown. She wore black jeans and a pink t-shirt with heart-shaped polka dots. Kim was dressed like a banker, Missy thought, taking in the black suit and light blue blouse, and her hair was pulled back in a neat, low ponytail anchored just north of Antarctica.

"I found them!" Mahdavi, smiling from ear to ear, said to Danny and Missy. Megan and Kim looked shocked as they took in the scene. Kim let go of Mahdavi's hand and covered her ears.

"Our new band uniforms were supposed to be here in time for today, but they never arrived," Danny explained, shouting over the cacophony. "Our band director was sure they would be here on time since the uniform company assured us they would be here this morning. We just found out that the plane they were on got delayed. Now, they say the uniforms won't get here until NEXT week!" Danny took a deep breath and continued, "Anyway, we never took out these old uniforms before today and we're finding they are in a terrible state—missing buttons, broken zippers, moth holes and stains. And we don't even think there are enough for everyone."

"What does the band director think?" Megan asked.

"He expected us to wear new uniforms," Mahdavi answered, spinning around to show off her half uniform, "I had on a jean skirt and fringed t-shirt. Most of us came dressed in really casual clothes. But he said that we could just wear what we came in."

Danny made a face. "We just don't think that looks very nice." Danny put his arm around Mahdavi, "So, we're trying to figure out what to do!"

"OMG!" Kim covered her face with her hands to avoid looking at the commotion around the room. "I can't even look." She cleared her throat, then said, "I'm really sorry about all this, but we have the math competition starting in an hour. And I think we need to focus on that."

Surprised by Kim's comments, Megan, Missy, Danny and Mahdavi stared blankly at her.

"Oh-kaaaay," said Danny crossing his arms and sticking out his hip. "We just thought y'all might wanna help." Danny reached out to Missy and Mahdavi. "We are the Figures and Icons!"

"Of course!" Missy responded, looking away from Kim and back around the room. "Let's see what we have to work with." Missy walked around the band room and took a quick inventory. She counted the number of band members and the individual uniform pieces. Surely, they could find a solution using the pieces they had! Missy stepped up to the band director and whispered something in his ear. The band director nodded and Missy walked back to Danny and her friends.

11 complete uniforms =
11 pants
11 jackets

Plus 3 extra jackets

"Danny, can you gather up all the uniforms and put all the usable pieces into piles?" Missy directed. "And, Mahdavi, please find out who wore jeans or pants today."

In a matter of minutes, with the help of the band members, Missy and her friends had sorted all the band pants, jackets and hats and found they had eleven complete uniforms plus three jackets that needed only minor repairs and could be worn as-is today. The other pieces were too tattered to be wearable.

"If each band member who wore jeans only wears a band jacket and everyone who wore shorts or skirts just wears the pants, you can stretch out the usable items and you'll still look like one band with matching uniforms," Missy remarked. "Fourteen jackets and eleven pants will more than cover twenty-two people."

Danny's eyes bugged out. "Really?!" he said. The girls looked at his current state of dress and giggled. "You will really need to wear the band pants," Mahdavi concluded.

"Well, you'll have to figure out who has appropriate pants and shirts and then shuffle things around and maybe trade some items between you," Missy said. "But I think you can do it!"

"Math to the rescue!" Ms. Jameson stepped into the room and approached the mathletes. She wore a navy blue pant suit with a crisp white blouse and low-heeled matching navy shoes. Ms. Jameson even wore make-up and had her hair in a bun. She had a large golden brooch of a Pi symbol pinned to her blazer collar and a red scarf tied neatly around her neck. Ms. Jameson shepherded the girls out of the band room commenting, "I'm glad I found you. We are getting ready to take our seats for the competition!"

Missy's head was overflowing with ideas. If the old band uniforms were getting replaced, they were probably going into the recycling bin. She hoped they could be donated to the fashion club. There was so much fabric to mine from them, not to mention all the buttons, zippers and trim! As Missy walked down the hall, new designs danced in her head.

Missy, Megan, Kim and Ms. Jameson entered one of the backstage practice rooms. The CHAPS mathletes silently sat in various positions around the tiny room, except Peter who was pacing around in the limited floor space surrounding them. The atmosphere felt heavy. It seemed so much quieter and more somber and serious in this room compared to the band room. Missy wondered if the rest of mathletes even thought math was fun.

Missy noticed how the mathletes on her team had dressed for the day, some casual and some downright professional, like Kim. She wished they had uniforms of their own to wear in order to show they all belonged to the same team. Even though she loved her OOTD, and thought some other outfits looked great too, the whole team looked like a random bunch of kids. Missy imagined they could look more cohesive in some kind of uniform. She filed that thought away to bring up to Ms. Jameson after the competition.

Missy and Megan looked around for an empty spot to sit down on the floor. Kim quickly took a seat in a space by the door.

"OK, mathletes! Today is OUR day!" Ms. Jameson cheered and everyone looked up.

"That's right," Peter said jumping up and pumping his fist in the air. Just then another mathlete stood up and Peter mis-stepped and tripped. He went down saying "Oomph." He flailed out his arms and flopped to the floor in a Superman pose. He quickly recovered, and was helped to his feet by Missy and Megan who were passing by.

"Uh. Thanks," Peter said surprised. Then he blushed, seeing that he was holding hands with two girls.

Relieved that he was okay, the room filled with laughter. Peter smiled and pretended to reenact his superhero crash. That broke the tension, and the chatter and excitement levels rose. Ms. Jameson gathered them together, and the team lined up to head to the auditorium. Maybe these mathletes did love math as much as she did, Missy decided. Missy wished the math team got the same support as other CHAPS teams.

The mathletes took their designated seats beside all the other teams from schools around the county. Missy twisted around in her chair and scanned the growing crowd. She saw Ivy from Fairmount Prep and a few other familiar faces from other school competitions. Strangely, Missy even thought she spotted world-renowned fashion designer Sarah DeMott standing next to Chris in the mezzanine! The famous designer had judged Missy's first fashion competition of the year. Missy remembered that she had an awesome sense of style.

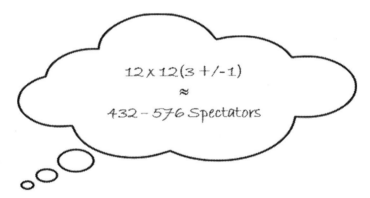

$$12 \times 12(3 +/- 1)$$
$$\approx$$
$$432 - 576 \text{ Spectators}$$

Missy continued scanning. AJ and G-ma had joined Mr. Maker in the audience. She made a mental note of where her dad was sitting after spotting him and AJ waving wildly to her from the back of the auditorium. Missy was thrilled they could all be there to cheer her and the CHAPS mathletes on. *Three or more friends or family members per mathlete times twelve school teams meant there were at least 432 spectators!* Not bad for an academic event, Missy thought to herself.

AJ held up a sign that said, "Go M³! Go CHAPS!" Missy smiled to herself knowing only AJ would have thought to make a sign just for her.

The CHAPS Marching Band expertly performed their rendition of "When the Saints Go Marching In" as the remaining students and spectators settled in their seats. They followed that up with the National Anthem and led the students and their families in the pledge of allegiance. As they exited the auditorium, they marched playing "The Ants Go Marching Two by Two." Missy laughed at the math reference and settled into her seat. When the band had fully exited, something amazing happened. Sarah DeMott stepped up to the center stage microphone. Missy's jaw flopped open. She couldn't believe that her favorite designer of all-time was here, at her school, hosting a math competition!

Missy took in every detail of Sarah DeMott's outfit from her pointy-toed, thigh-high, black leather boots with giant buttons running down the outsides like beetles standing at attention, to her green, white and blue plaid skirt that skimmed the top of her boots, to her fitted cable knit sweater with three-quarter-length sleeves and v-neck neckline. Topping it all off was a mini fedora floating atop her blond hair. It tilted slightly above her left eye. Missy wondered how many bobby pins had been used to anchor it in place to keep it secure from the effects of gravity.

Miss DeMott began speaking and Missy leaned forward on the edge of her seat. "Wow! That was a great performance by the Cherry Hill Band. Let's give them another round of applause!"

Everyone clapped, then Miss DeMott said, "Thank you all for coming! My name is Sarah DeMott, and I am here to welcome all of you—students, teachers, parents and supporters—to this exciting STEM event! Science, technology, engineering, and math are mind-opening subjects and learning them well prepares us for many opportunities in life."

Missy listened intently and thought she was hearing a recording of her own father's words. If it had not been Sarah DeMott speaking them, she might have rolled her eyes and tuned out completely. How many times had her father said that studying math and science were the keys to a successful future? She had long ago lost count!

Miss DeMott continued, "As many of you know, I am a fashion designer, but you may not know that I am also a mathlete. I have loved math for as long as I can remember, especially geometry. And, while I am a designer today, my first career was as a mechanical engineer. I love shapes and patterns. I adore all the calculations and formulas that we use in design and engineering and architecture to make those shapes and patterns fit perfectly together. I am thrilled to be your host today." She went on to discuss the day's event and the rules of the competition. Then Miss DeMott introduced the judges and the competition began.

Missy was stunned. Her favorite designer was a mathlete AND an engineer?! Missy suddenly had a new perspective. $M^3$ could be a designer and a math Olympian and whatever else she wanted to be!

"Math is awesome and so is Sarah DeMott," Missy said to herself smiling ear to ear.

Based on their ranking and a series of coin tosses, CHAPS sat out the first several rounds of the Math Olympics. Missy was glad for that because it allowed her to see exactly how the competition worked. She had practiced with the CHAPS mathletes and had watched them scrimmage before, but she had never participated in or watched an actual live event.

Missy observed that each individual on the team answered one math problem, rotating back and forth across two teams per round. The competition proceeded in timed rounds, and every round included individual questions followed by more complex team questions. Team questions required the whole team to work out a response and to agree before presenting their final answer within a specified time limit. Each question had a number of points associated with it, and the team with the most points at the end of the round advanced to the next level of the competition. Missy noticed how rapt all the attending mathletes were. Each raced to solve the problems on their own in their heads or by scratching notes on index cards or notebooks. Missy could tell from frustrated actions like head slapping and fist banging whenever someone got a wrong answer. In three rounds, Missy had not missed one of the questions as she answered along to herself!

CHAPS took the stage for the fourth round, and won by two points, advancing to the next level. The CHAPS mathletes also won the following round and advanced with two other teams to the final round, which was scheduled after lunch. The CHAPS Marching Band returned and performed a classic rock mash-up. Then they marched down the aisles, and led the audience to the cafeteria. Each of the math teams reported to a different room where pizza, juice and water, and cut-up vegetables were served to them for lunch.

As the auditorium was emptying out from the main doors behind all the seats, the mathletes were led out through the backstage exit doors. Missy saw Chris approach Sarah DeMott in the corner of the stage. Miss DeMott touched his arm when she spoke to Chris, and Missy felt a jolt of electricity in her own arm. The two seemed so friendly, like they knew each other well.

The CHAPS mathletes regrouped in the small practice room where they had met in the morning. It smelled of hot pizza. Missy's mouth watered when she stepped inside.

"Great job!" Ms. Jameson congratulated the team. "I'm so proud of all of you!" she said. "Now let's relax and hydrate and enjoy lunch! We have forty-five minutes before the finals begin."

From the doorway, Peter looked at Ms. Jameson and raised his eyebrows in a question. She signaled back to him with a nod and a wink. "Gooooo CHAPS!" he said, and everyone echoed in reply. Then the team lined up to get their lunches.

*Three pizzas with eight slices for twelve students meant everyone could have two slices each.* After Missy took a slice and some carrots and celery, she looked around the room for a place to sit and saw that Kim and Megan were on opposite sides of the room. Missy finally made eye contact with Megan, who motioned for Missy to sit down next to her. Missy carefully wound her way through the crowded room hoping not to have an epic fall like Peter had done earlier that day. When she made it safely to Megan, she said "Whew!" and carefully folded her legs to sit in the space next to her friend.

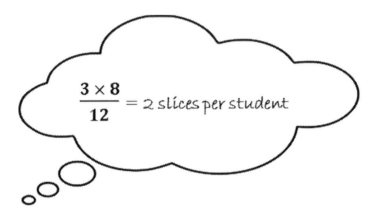

"Can you believe Sarah DeMott is our host? Can you even believe that she is a mathlete?" Missy asked Megan.

"Totally!" Megan replied.

"Really?" Missy said, considering the facts. "She's so glamorous and pretty and her designs are so AH-MAZING. I guess I never expected someone could love both math and fashion!"

Now it was Megan's turn to be surprised. "Seriously?" she asked. "Did you ever look in the mirror?"

Missy smiled. "I guess I just never saw myself that way. But, I really am enjoying the competition. I should have joined the team sooner."

Missy took a bite of pizza and absorbed the quiet vibe of the room. She wanted to ask Megan why she and Kim were not sitting together, but everyone was eating so the room was virtually silent, and Missy did not want to make a big deal out of it—especially if it was nothing.

"Mmmm. Good pizza," Megan commented, wiping her face with a napkin.

"Yep," Missy responded. "Tastes like Big Jim's. That's my family's favorite."

As people finished their first slice, several students lined up to take a second slice and the chatter picked up. Missy took the opportunity to ask Megan about Kim. "It's simple," Megan said. "She's mad because of the band stuff this morning. Kim didn't want to get involved because she said it was a big distraction, but I wanted to help, and I said she should come along too when Mahdavi came to us and explained the situation."

"Oh. I guess it was a distraction, but it really helped calm my nerves," Missy said. "And, I'm glad we could help the band. They have been awesome today!

They played so well, their uniforms hardly mattered, but I do think they looked good."

"I know it, right? Anyway, I'm glad we could help too, though that band room was crazy," Megan said and smiled at Missy. "Hey—it's great to have another girl on the team! It's super that you could fill in this weekend. We were so happy that we didn't have to forfeit the competition."

"Thanks," Missy said. "I'm really inspired by Miss DeMott! I think I would like to join the team if there's room for me!"

"That's super! We should tell Ms. J!" Megan exclaimed.

Missy nodded. "And, we should talk to Kim. I feel bad that she's mad about this morning. By the way, whatever happened to the bullying situation?" Missy asked Megan.

Megan had just taken a sip of water and swallowed wrong. She coughed and sputtered. The question seemed to have caught her off guard. "Oh. That. Someone posted on SocialMe that I should quit the math club. At first I was so mad. Then I just got sad and a little bit scared."

"OMG. Really?" Missy asked. "That's awful!"

"Yeah," Megan continued. "I wasn't sure what to do about it. My parents talked to the principal. They took the message down and I haven't seen anything like it since. It was a mess. I was thinking about quitting even though I didn't want to quit. And, Kim didn't want me to quit and leave her as the only girl on the team." Megan looked across the room and finger waved at Kim who was sitting alone by the door. Kim waved back and gave a tentative smile. She pushed herself up to her feet and joined the other two girls.

"Hey," Kim said.

"Hey," Missy and Megan said in unison.

"Jinx," Missy whispered. "Later," she said referring to finishing the game. "We were just talking about SocialMe bullies."

"Anyway," Megan continued, "I worked so hard and I improved a lot in my math skills. It was not easy at first, but I started to really like it. So, I'm glad Ms. Jameson and the principal could help, although we still don't know who was behind the mean messages." Megan looked at Kim who smiled in earnest. "All I know is that they just stopped. So, I'm glad that I took your advice and talked to a teacher! Ms. J listened and helped me get through everything."

Missy tried not to think back to the year before when she was bullied for being a good student—and especially for showing her math skills. Yet, it all came flooding back to her. In her case, two students had been identified and expelled from school. Then, the whole school attended anti-bullying workshops and

Missy had hoped it was over forever. The thought of a bully hurting her friends upset her. She would be there for them and help in any way that she could.

While Megan was talking, Missy pulled out her phone and brought up her SocialMe and showed the girls the message from that morning. "At first, I was really upset at seeing that terrible nickname again, but I decided to embrace it. I'm 'M-cubed'. I think it's sassy!"

Kim raised her eyebrows, "You should probably mention it to Ms. Jameson, you know, just so she knows."

"You're right. I will. Even though I don't think it's bullying in my case," Missy said, and then she made her way over to the trash can to throw away her paper plate.

On her way back to her friends, Missy first walked over to Ms. Jameson who was sitting at a makeshift desk consisting of a folding chair stacked with boxes of copy paper. She was eating a pre-packaged salad and crackers.

"Hey there, Missy! Great job so far. Are you having fun?" Ms. Jameson asked.

"It's been great," Missy said, looking down at her feet wondering how to approach the subject.

"So, what's up, kiddo? Do you need something?" Ms. Jameson asked.

"Actually," Missy started. "I wanted to show you something. I'm not upset— any more—but with all the cyberbullying, I just wanted you to know about this comment on my SocialMe page."

Ms. Jameson stood up and walked with Missy into the hallway. There, she took Missy's phone from her outstretched hand and read the posting along with Missy's response and the subsequent comments. "You handled that very well," Ms. Jameson said. "I'm sorry to see any name-calling—even if it's all in good fun. I promise to investigate it and we'll have the comments taken down." She shook her head and handed Missy her phone back. "Thank you for showing this to me. On the plus side, it looks like your friends are really supporting you!"

"Okay. Thanks," Missy said as she stepped back into the room. "Oh. By the way, I think I want to join the math team more permanently, if that's alright," Missy headed across the room to where her friends sat.

"That's wonderful," Ms. Jameson called to her as she made her way across the room.

"Hey, Missy, I just read some of the comments out there on SocialMe," Kim said.

"You've got quite a fan club, M-cubed," Megan said, using her fingers to make quote signs.

"Do I?" Missy asked looking at her phone and scrolling through. "Wow! I guess I do!" Missy was thrilled to see her friends had posted even more comments and responses supporting her.

As the team finished eating and everyone started cleaning up their cups, plates and napkins, Peter rallied the team, and called for a cheer. Missy led them with the mantra from her dad, "Math is awesome and so are we! Goooooo CHAPS!" The team repeated her cheer as they marched out of the room and down the hallway.

The stage had been rearranged to accommodate the three teams that had made it to the finals. The tables were set in a u-shaped configuration with the microphone still set up in the center of the stage.

Chris walked past Missy muttering to himself, bumping her shoulder as she took her seat. He was dressed in black from head to toe and carried a length of cable over his left shoulder. He held an oversized walkie-talkie in his right hand. His long hair hung straight down revealing only one eye. Missy's heart fluttered. Chris sidestepped several other mathletes to avoid a collision as he headed down the steps and into the side aisle rushing toward the mezzanine.

Missy wondered what the hurry was all about just as Sarah DeMott spoke into the microphone and feedback tore through the overhead speakers. The high-pitched sound had students and supporters covering their ears with their hands or plugging them with their fingertips. Missy noticed AJ had held onto her posterboard sign when she covered her ears, so it now formed a strange, giant bonnet over her head.

After a loud click, the feedback ended and Miss DeMott shouted to the audience that they were having some technical difficulties and that the band would perform one last time before the final round. The CHAPS Marching Band started playing in the hallway, then they marched into and around the auditorium playing "Seventy-six Trombones" from the Music Man musical.

"What a perfect song!" Missy thought and found herself humming along to the catchy tune. She looked for and spotted Chris in the mezzanine waving signals to someone backstage. The song wrapped up and the band exited to roaring applause. No microphones were needed for that team! Missy watched Chris and smiled when she saw him give the thumbs-up signal. She knew it was for his AV contact backstage, but she felt like it was aimed directly at her.

Sarah DeMott spoke into the now working mic and reviewed the rules. "Congratulations to our three finalist teams! What an exciting day we have had so far! At the end of this round, the highest scoring team will be named champion of the Math Olympics!" she explained.

For the final round, CHAPS was seated stage left, Fairmount Prep was stage right, and St. Mark's Academy sat at the center table. Missy waved across the stage to Ivy who winked at her and waved back. The Fairmount Prep team all wore red golf shirts with the school logo on the front and the students' last names in yellow letters across the back. St. Mark's mathletes wore their school uniform jackets with white shirts and khaki pants and skirts. Missy looked down the line at the CHAPS mathletes. She envisioned them all wearing gray t-shirts each with a different white math notation, CHAPS Knights graphic, and their names imprinted on the back. *Ten dollars per t-shirt for each mathlete and Ms. J.* Missy wondered if the math club had at least $130 in their treasury to fund her uniform idea.

Silence settled over the stage as Miss DeMott read out the questions. The mathletes solved a plethora of problems. One after the other no one got a wrong answer. Missy imagined the final round might last until midnight. Then, St. Mark's got eliminated. They lost two points on a team question when one student blurted out a correct answer without the agreement of his teammates. Ms. Jameson had cautioned them about presenting answers in the team challenges, so Peter made sure everyone agreed on the final answer even when time was short.

The whole competition came down to a duel between CHAPS and Fairmount Prep! The two teams had perfect scores for the day.

"Okay! Great job mathletes," Miss DeMott announced. "We have one last question and the first team to respond with the correct answer will win the Math Olympics. Are you ready?" she asked and everyone nodded.

Missy heard someone in the audience crinkling a wrapper through the quiet.

"I am designing a dress for a gala," Miss DeMott said, beginning the math problem. "The dress is made of eight identical right triangles plus two identical rectangles. I also need 15% more fabric to account for fittings and adjustments. How many yards of fabric do I need to purchase to construct my dress? And, if I don't have to make any adjustments, how much may become waste?" Sarah DeMott shared the dimensions and set the time clock.

As Miss DeMott asked the question, Missy saw shapes lining up in her mind's eye. She quickly realized that the four right triangles came together to measure the same size as the rectangle. Missy multiplied it all out. She determined that seventy-two inches or two yards of material measuring thirty-six inches wide would need to be purchased, and two yards by six inches could be waste. Though in Missy's mind, there was always another project to be made from any scraps.

"Got it!" Missy said, and Peter rang the buzzer. Without him asking, the whole team nodded. Missy presented the solution.

"Correct!" Miss DeMott declared. "Congratulations to Cherry Hill Academy and Preparatory School!"

"Wahoo!" Missy heard her father's cheer from the back of the auditorium as her team surrounded her and patted her on the back.

The mathletes lined up and congratulated the other teams on their well-fought math battle. Each of the finalists received a medal, and the CHAPS mathletes received a team trophy too.

"Well done!" Ms. Jameson shook everyone's hands as they filed back into the tiny practice room. She gave Missy a squeeze around her shoulders as she passed by. "I am so proud of you. You all did a great job!"

"Hey, M-cubed," Peter called to Missy. "Thanks for helping us today. I hope you will consider joining the team."

"I will! Ms. Jameson has promised me a spot! And, I can't wait for the next meet," Missy announced, and everyone high-fived.

Missy took a selfie with the team that she noticed was photo-bombed by Danny and Mahdavi still dressed in their band uniforms. The two had slipped into the room amidst the celebration. Missy posted the photo to her SocialMe page with the hashtags mathmakers and CHAPSforthewin. Then she gathered up her coat and backpack to leave. When Missy turned around to say goodbye to her friends, she saw Chris at the door with Sarah DeMott. She felt her face flush with color.

"OMG. OMG," Megan said, jumping in place and tugging on Missy's coat. "That's Sarah DeMott!"

"I know it!" said Missy.

Ms. Jameson cleared her throat. "And, here's a special surprise. Miss Sarah DeMott would like to congratulate you in person."

"Thank you, Jenn." she said to Ms. Jameson. "Great job, mathletes. I'm so honored to be here at CHAPS. I am really impressed by all the students today, and I hope you continue your math studies! Good luck to you all!"

"Miss DeMott has time for a few questions if anyone would like to talk to her," Ms. Jameson announced.

Missy had so many questions: How did you go from engineering to fashion? What did you like to do in middle school? Who's your favorite designer?

As the students stepped up to ask their questions, Missy noticed Chris was lingering in the doorway. When she looked at him, he smiled and nodded at her. She bravely walked over and said hello.

"Hey. Good job on the competition," Chris said. "Did you see I gave you a thumbs-up at halftime?"

Missy blushed. "I did!" she said, and then she scratched her head. "So. Wait a sec. Do you know Miss DeMott? You two looked so chummy today and now you're here—with her."

Chris tossed his head back, flipping his hair and briefly revealing a glimpse into both eyes. "Oh yeah. She's my aunt. My mom's sister."

"That's super," Missy said. "Wow! You're so lucky to know her. She's amazing—electrifying, really."

Chris nodded, "Yeah. She's cool."

"Okay. Ready?" Miss DeMott said over Missy's shoulder to Chris.

"Mmhmm," Chris said. "This is Missy," Chris introduced the two.

Missy gushed, "OMG! Wow! You're my inspiration." Missy turned to shake Sarah DeMott's hand. "I love your mini fedora! How did you get it to stay in place?"

"Thank you, Missy. Between you and me, I used seven hairpins and some double-sided tape—a designer's favorite insurance policy! By the way, you are quite an inspiration yourself. Nice job on that last question, and on your outfit. That skirt is divine!"

Missy beamed at the fashion icon nearly forgetting how to speak, "I-I made it," she finally said.

"The shapes, the pattern. The geometry of your skirt is like a poem. It's a great design. I hope I'll be seeing you again! Ta-ta," Miss DeMott said. She looped her arm through Chris's and they headed out.

Missy stared after them, watching them disappear down the hall. Without turning back, Chris put his arm out to the side making a thumbs-up signal with his hand that Missy knew he aimed directly at her.

## FASHION HACK: BLANKET SHAWL HOW-TO

1. Find a favorite old blanket or towel that you want to upcycle. It should be a long rectangle.

2. Sew or staple the corners 1 to 2 and 3 to 4 together to create a simple shawl. Turn the garment inside-out to hide your sewing or staples. Embellish with buttons, ribbons or paint.

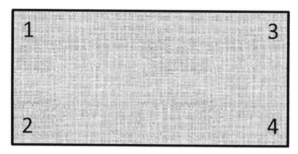

3. Put your arms through the newly formed sleeves (the openings created though corners 1 + 2 and corners 3 + 4).

# Pi for All

Missy, AJ and the Makers celebrated the CHAPS win over General Tso's Chicken and Hot and Sour Soup at Missy's favorite Chinese restaurant, *Amazing Chow*. Mr. Maker, AJ and G-ma shared the high points of the competition from the audience perspective, while Missy relived the suspenseful moments the team experienced when the microphones stopped working after lunch. They all laughed at the image Missy painted of AJ's posterboard bonnet.

Just as the fortune cookies came out, Ms. Jameson appeared. "Matt! I'm so sorry I couldn't join you sooner," she said to Mr. Maker. "I had some investigating to do! And, I hoped to have some news to share."

Missy and AJ exchanged perplexed looks.

"Do join us, Jennifer!" Mr. Maker said smiling widely. He leaned back and pulled a chair from a neighboring table and slid it between himself and G-ma.

Ms. Jameson settled into the chair and gave G-ma a kiss by way of greeting and said hello to the girls.

"Jenny, would you like to order some dinner? I'm sure they can get you something quickly," G-ma said.

"Oh. No thank you," Ms. Jameson said.

"Well, congratulations, dearie! The kids were great today—and so were you!" G-ma added.

"Thank you! You are right. The students did an outstanding job. I could not be more proud! The only blight on our day was the cyberbullying incident," Ms. Jameson added.

© Melissa A. Borza and CA 2017
M. A. Borza, *Fashion Figures*, DOI 10.1007/978-1-4842-2274-4_11

Missy's jaw dropped open. She had not said anything to her dad and she hoped the whole thing would just fade away.

"You okay, Missy?" Mr. Maker asked.

Missy made a show of opening her fortune cookie and popping it into her mouth. "Mmm hmmm," she answered. AJ nudged her leg from under the table and looked at her with raised eyebrows.

Mr. Maker turned his attention to Ms. Jameson, "What's this about cyberbullying?"

"A few of the mathletes reported hurtful posts on their SocialMe pages earlier this school year. With CHAPS' zero tolerance policy, I was shocked to see another post today with name-calling," Ms. Jameson explained. "Missy showed me the comment calling her 'Missy-Math-Maker' and I raised the flag and let the principal know we needed to start an investigation."

"Oh no!" AJ jumped up from the table. "I'm so sorry." She pulled Missy's arm and grabbed her hand. "That was me. I meant to cheer you on and let everyone know you were helping the team today and that you'd be great. OMG. It wasn't to bully you. Missy, I'm sorry if I hurt you," AJ said and dropped back into her chair sobbing into her hands. "Plus I was in a rush. I was making your poster and getting out to practice. Then catching a ride with G-ma."

"Wow," Missy said. "I thought it was weirdly supportive, but since you called me out using the name I hate, it hurt my feelings. I thought you were an anonymous bully. I worked so hard this year to show people that I'm not just about math—that I love other things like fashion—and wow. I don't know what to say," Missy said.

"Please forgive me," AJ said to Missy. "I'm really sorry that I hurt your feelings. I would never do that on purpose. I posted it from my cousin's account when I didn't have my phone with me. It's not anonymous. Oh Missy! You're my best friend!"

"Okay. Okay," G-ma said. "Everyone take a deep breath."

"I-I forgive you," Missy said. "I know you meant it in the best possible way."

AJ leaned over and side-hugged Missy. "I'm ready to face my consequences," AJ said to Ms. Jameson.

"Girls, I think you both agree this was not the cyberbullying that we initially thought it was," Ms. Jameson said and the two nodded. "So, we will close the investigation and move on from here. Agreed? We do have a more serious investigation going on that resulted in losing one member from the math team."

Missy and AJ nodded again.

Mr. Maker scratched his head and straightened his pink and blue plaid bow tie. "I've never told you this Missy, but I had a nickname in school too, didn't I Jenn? Mom, do you remember?"

Ms. Jameson's face lit up, "Matt! I had completely forgotten about that."

"Oh, sonny!" G-ma said. "Didn't your friends call you Matty-Math-Maker?"

"They sure did!" Mr. Maker said proudly. "To me, it was a badge of honor. With my interests in math and science, I have built a successful career as a software engineer."

Missy rolled her eyes. She never knew about her dad's nickname, but she had heard this math-path story many times before. Mr. Maker liked to remind Missy that studying math and science opened doors to wealth and success. And, after hearing Sarah DeMott earlier that day, Missy was starting to believe it!

Mr. Maker reached for a fortune cookie, cracked it open and read his fortune. "Listen to this," he said. "Math teachers love Pi for dessert."

"It does not say that!" Ms. Jameson grabbed the tiny strip of paper from Mr. Maker.

"I swear, it does!" Mr. Maker said putting his hand over his heart.

Ms. Jameson re-read the fortune. "It really does say that! Okay, then. I guess I will have some pie, after all!" she said.

"Make that pie for everyone," Mr. Maker said to the waiter.

# Afterword

Inspiration comes from crazy places. The inspiration for Missy Maker and this book comes from my enduring love of math and science, my love of learning and my longtime desire to write a book for young people. When I think about my early education, I have lovely memories of attending St. Cecelia's Catholic Elementary School. There I was taught Earth Science along with multiplication and division by nuns and lay teachers.

One of my fondest memories is the exact moment when long division just clicked for me—when all the times' tables' memorization finally paid off. Sister Ann taught third grade math at St. Cecelia's. One sunny afternoon she spent showing the class how to set up long division statements and how to work out the answers. At first, it seemed so strange, so foreign. I didn't believe it could work at all. What kind of math sentence was this? And why did we have to use multiplication and subtraction in division? Then it clicked. It all made sense, and I begged for extra homework. How strange is THAT? I begged for homework just to have more long division problems to practice solving!

While many of my friends never believed or even understood my true love for long division, they did appreciate my mean math skills! To this day, I still enjoy a really juicy long division problem. Don't you?

I poured that love of math (and so much more!) into my character, Missy Maker. I hope you enjoyed meeting her, and I hope you will come along with us for another adventure. Missy Maker has many great escapades ahead of her.

© Melissa A. Borza and CA 2017
M. A. Borza, *Fashion Figures*, DOI 10.1007/978-1-4842-2274-4

Printed in the United States
By Bookmasters